THE WORLD'S GREATEST COLLECTION OF DAD JOKES

MORE THAN 500 OF THE PUNNIEST JOKES DADS LOVE TO TELL

Compiled by
Glenn Hascall

BARBOUR BOOKS
An Imprint of Barbour Publishing, Inc.

Published by Barbour Books, an imprint of Barbour Publishing, Inc.,
P.O. Box 719, Uhrichsville, Ohio 44683, www.barbourbooks.com

*Our mission is to publish and distribute inspirational products offering
exceptional value and biblical encouragement to the masses.*

Member of the
Evangelical Christian
Publishers Association

Printed in the United States of America.

INTRODUCTION

Who would tell a joke that's so bad it's good? Dad—that's who.

Dad jokes are dedicated to those proud fathers who once dreamed of being a stand-up comic but settled for bringing their families to a place of groans, unanswered pleas to stop, and a single word of disgust, *"Daaaaaaaaaaaad!"*

Brave fathers have embraced their inner storyteller for decades. This usually happens when their youngest offspring hears their first "dad" joke and laughs, laughs again, and shares the joke with their older sibling. They say, "Good one, Dad" before anyone can help them realize the mistake they've made.

You don't have to be a dad to find humor in this book. Share these jokes freely in either an attempt to bring humor to the life of those you love or annoy them mercilessly. There probably won't be much middle ground.

You can be eight years old and chuckle until tears squirt from your eyeballs. You can be fifteen and think some are lame, but will continue reading anyway. You can be a mom, grandma, uncle, or niece. You could even be a dad in waiting, and like a moth to the flame you'll take each joke and laugh or groan, but at some point, you'll share the joke. You can't help yourself. It's part of the "dad joke code."

Don't be surprised if this book ultimately is dog-eared, marked up, and a bit ragged. It's a long-term guide to the best of the worst.

Long live dad jokes.

CONTENTS

1. IN HINDSIGHT

He will yet fill your mouth with laughter
and your lips with shouts of joy.
JOB 8:21 NIV

Objects in mirror look older
than they used to appear.
JON LAWHON

— — — — —

"My eighty-five-year-old grandfather gets up early every morning to jog two miles."

"That's amazing! What does he do in the afternoon?"

"The last mile."

■ ■ ■

"When Abraham Lincoln was your age," a man said to his lazy teenage son, "he was chopping wood, plowing, and hunting for food."

"When he was your age," the boy responded, "he was president of the United States."

■ ■ ■

Is it too much to hope that my good cholesterol will be a positive influence on my bad cholesterol?

"I think the Smiths are suffering from age-related stress," a woman said of her neighbors.

"What do you mean?" asked her husband.

"He won't act his age, and she won't admit hers."

■ ■ ■

A man had lived in the country all his life. He and his family were visiting the city for the first time. They were impressed by almost everything they saw, especially the skyscrapers. In the lobby of one tall building, the man and his son watched with amazement as two shiny, silver walls slid open before them, revealing a small room behind.

"What is that, Pop?" the boy asked.

"I've never seen anything like it, son," the man replied. "I don't know what it is."

At that moment, a stooped old lady shuffled into the tiny room and pressed a button on the wall. The shiny, silver doors closed, and a panel of numbers above the doors lit up—1, 2, 3, all the way to 10.

Then the numbers reversed direction—10, 9, 8, 7, 6, 5, 4, 3, 2, 1.

The shiny, silver walls slid open again, and a beautiful young woman stepped out.

"Son," the man said, staring, "go and get your ma."

Two would-be fishermen rented a boat, and one caught a large fish. "We should mark the spot," he said.

The second man drew a large X in the bottom of the boat with a black marker. "That's no good," said the first man. "Next time out, we may not get the same boat."

■ ■ ■

An elderly couple had finally saved enough money for a trip around the world. They had never flown on a plane before and were eager to experience air travel.

As they arrived in Chicago, they rolled to a stop, and a little red truck drove up and refueled the plane.

They next landed in Seattle, and again, a red truck pulled up to refuel the plane.

"These planes make great time, don't they, dear?" asked the husband.

"Yes, they do," replied the wife. "And that little red truck doesn't do too bad, either!"

A woman in Brooklyn decided to prepare her will and make her final requests. She told her pastor she had two final requests. First, she wanted to be cremated, and second, she wanted her ashes scattered all over her favorite department store.

The pastor found that odd and asked, "Why there?"

"So I'll be sure my daughters visit me twice a week."

■ ■ ■

Two old friends met one day after many years. The one who had attended college was now quite successful. The other had not attended college and never had much ambition.

The successful one said, "How has everything been going with you?"

"Well, one day, I closed my eyes, opened my Bible, and pointed. When I opened my eyes, I read the word *oil*. So I invested in oil, and the wells flowed. Then another day I dropped my finger on another word, and it was *gold*. So I invested in gold, and those mines really produced. Now I have millions of dollars."

The successful friend was so impressed that he ran home, grabbed his Bible, closed his eyes, flipped it open, and dropped his finger on a page. He opened his eyes and read the words *Chapter Eleven*.

Ten Ways to Tell You're Growing Older

1. Everything hurts, and what doesn't hurt doesn't work.
2. The gleam in your eye is from the sun hitting your bifocals.
3. You get winded playing cards.
4. You join a health club and don't go.
5. You know all the answers, but nobody asks you the questions.
6. You look forward to a dull evening.
7. You need glasses to find your glasses.
8. Your knees buckle, but your belt won't.
9. Your back goes out more than you do.
10. You have too much room in the house and not enough in the medicine chest.

■ ■ ■

A teenager told his father, "There's trouble with the car. It has water in the carburetor."

The father looked confused and said, "Water in the carburetor? That's ridiculous."

But the son insisted. "The car has water in the carburetor."

His father started to get a little agitated. "You don't even know what a carburetor is," he said. "I'll check it out. Where is the car?"

"In the pool."

Jim always read the obituaries in the newspaper. All his friends knew of his habit, so they decided to play a trick on him. They submitted his name and picture to the column.

The next morning, Jim picked up the newspaper, turned to the obituaries, and saw his name and picture with a biography underneath. Shocked, he ran to the telephone and called his friend Fred. "Do you have today's newspaper?" he asked. "You do? Turn to the obituaries and tell me what you see halfway down the page."

After a pause, Fred said, "Hey, that's you, Jim! Um, where are you calling from?"

■ ■ ■

An elderly gentleman had serious hearing problems for a number of years. He went to the doctor and was fitted for a set of hearing aids that allowed the man to hear perfectly.

The elderly gentleman went back in a month to the doctor, and the doctor said, "Your hearing is perfect. Your family must be really pleased you can hear again."

The gentleman replied, "Oh, I haven't told my family yet. I just sit around and listen to their conversations. I've changed my will five times!"

An elderly woman in her nineties had a visitor from her church come to see her at the nursing home.

"How are you?" the visitor asked.

"Oh," said the elderly woman, "I'm just worried sick!"

"You look like you're in good health. They take good care of you here, don't they?"

"Oh, yes, they take good care of me here."

"Do you have any pain?" the visitor asked.

"No, I can't say as I do," the elderly woman replied.

"Then what has you worried sick?" the visitor asked.

The elderly woman leaned in and explained, "All my closest friends have already died and gone to heaven. I'm sure they are all wondering where I went!"

■ ■ ■

Remember when. . .

 . . .an application was for employment?

 . . .a CD was a bank account?

 . . .a program was a show on television?

 . . .a web was a spider's home?

 . . .a hard drive was a long car ride?

 . . .memory was something you lost as you got older?

 . . .a keyboard was a piano?

 . . .a virus was the flu?

It was raining, the windshield had mud splattered on it, and the car had almost collided with another vehicle twice. The hitchhiker was beginning to wish that this driver hadn't picked him up.

"Don't you think you should wipe off the windshield?" asked the passenger.

"Oh, no," said the motorist with a smile. "That wouldn't do a bit of good. I left my glasses at home."

■ ■ ■

Four elderly ladies came into the pro shop after playing eighteen holes of golf. They appeared to be a bit exhausted. The pro asked, "Did you ladies have a good game today?"

The first lady said, "Well, I had four riders today."

The second lady said, "I had the most riders I've ever had. . .five."

The third lady said, "I did about the same as last time. I had seven."

The last lady said, "I beat my old record. I had ten riders today. Isn't that great?"

After they had gone into the ladies' locker room, another golfer who had overheard their conversation went to the pro and said, "I have been playing golf for thirty years and thought I knew all the terminology of the game, but what in the world is a rider?"

The pro said, "A rider occurs when you hit the ball far enough to get in the golf cart and ride to it."

The CEO of a large corporation was in a meeting with the board of directors. He presented his plan, although he knew that several of the board members would disagree.

"All in favor, say, 'Aye,' " said the CEO. "All opposed, say, 'I resign.' "

■ ■ ■

Two old buddies went fishing, and one lost his dentures over the side of the boat. His prankster friend removed his own false teeth, tied them on his line, and pretended he had caught them.

Unhooking the teeth, his grateful mate tried to put them into his mouth then hurled them into the lake with disgust. "They're not mine! They don't fit!"

■ ■ ■

A veteran of World War II applied for a job at a bank. The impersonal interviewer continued to ask question after question, scribbling notes, and never looking at the veteran.

"Most recent position?" asked the official.

"Supply officer," replied the applicant.

"Duration of employment?"

"Three and a half years."

"Reason for termination?"

The applicant stopped and thought for a moment then answered, "We won."

A mother's bachelor son invited her over for a meal. He had just gotten two new dogs and wanted his mom to see them.

When she sat down at the table, she noticed that the dishes were the dirtiest that she had ever seen in her life. "Have these dishes ever been washed?" she asked, running her fingers over the grit and grime.

"They're as clean as soap and water could get them," he answered. She felt a bit apprehensive but started eating anyway. The food was really delicious, and she said so, despite the dirty dishes.

When dinner was over, her son took the dishes, put them on the floor, whistled, and yelled, "Here, Soap! Here, Water!"

■ ■ ■

"What do you mean I'm not qualified?" demanded a job applicant. "I have an IQ of 150. I scored 1,480 on the SAT. I was magna cum laude in graduate school."

"Yes," replied the hiring supervisor, "but we don't really require intelligence around here."

■ ■ ■

I'm tired from my head down to my shoes. That's a pretty good distance because I'm in my man cave, and my shoes are in my bedroom.

One morning a little boy proudly surprised his grandmother with a cup of coffee he had made himself. He eagerly waited to hear the verdict on the quality of the coffee.

The grandmother had never in her life had such a bad cup of coffee, and as she forced down the last sip, she noticed three of those little green army guys in the bottom of the cup. She asked, "Honey, why would three little green army guys be in the bottom of my cup?"

Her grandson replied, "You know, Grammy, it's just like on television. 'The best part of waking up is soldiers in your cup.' "

■ ■ ■

The foreman laughed when a tiny old man in a plaid shirt applied for a job as a lumberjack.

"So you think you can be a lumberjack?" the boss asked. "What's your experience?"

"I've felled a million trees single-handedly," said the old man. "Ever hear of the Mojave Forest?"

"You mean the Mojave Desert," corrected the foreman.

"Sure—now!"

Martin had just received his brand-new driver's license. The family trooped out to the driveway and climbed into the car, with Martin in the driver's seat, ready to take them for a ride for the first time. His father was in the backseat, directly behind the new driver.

"I'll bet you're back there to get a change of scenery after all those months of sitting in the front seat, teaching me how to drive," said the boy to his father.

"Nope," came his father's reply, "I'm gonna sit here and kick the back of your seat as you drive, just like you've been doing to me all these years."

■ ■ ■

Three older ladies were driving down the highway at a very slow speed. A policeman pulled them over and explained that driving so slowly on the highway could be hazardous. The driver explained that she was following the posted limit: twenty miles per hour.

The policeman hid a smile, looking at the sign the woman had indicated. "Ma'am," he said, "that sign indicates that you are traveling on Highway 20."

"Well, that explains why Sally has been so quiet back there," the woman admitted. "We just turned off Highway 110."

An old businessman, near death, called for his brother to come to his side.

"Please see that I'm cremated," he told his brother.

"What should I do with your ashes?" his brother asked.

"I would like you to put them in an envelope and send them to the IRS with a note that says: 'Here. Now you have everything.' "

■ ■ ■

A policeman was on patrol when he came upon a line of cars stopped at a light with horns blasting. The light directing that lane of traffic was green. He pulled out of line and stopped alongside of the first car in line to see what the problem was.

The car was driven by an elderly woman. He asked her why she was stopped when the light was green.

She said, "Oh, because I'm on my way to my sister's house, which is that way," and she pointed to the right.

The motorcycle cop said, "Well go ahead! The light is green."

The elderly woman responded with, "Yes I know, but the sign under the light says Right Turn on Red."

"I'll just give you a warning this time," said the police officer to the beautiful young woman he had pulled over for speeding. He then handed over the slip of paper.

"Oh, thank you, Officer!" she said as she slipped it into her purse. "I can add this one to my collection!"

■ ■ ■

Three elderly sisters are sitting in the living room, chatting about various things. One sister says, "You know, I'm getting really forgetful. This morning, I was standing at the top of the stairs, and I couldn't remember whether I had just come up or was about to go down."

The second sister says, "You think that's bad? The other day, I was sitting on the edge of my bed, and I couldn't remember whether I was going to bed or had just woken up!"

The third sister smiles smugly. "Well, my memory's just as good as it's always been, knock on wood." She raps on the table. "You sit still. I'll answer the door."

Two American climbers were scaling an obscure peak in Alaska. They journeyed for three days and reached the summit, exhausted. They enjoyed their success and the beauty of the view then prepared for their descent.

"All right, give me the American flag so we can plant it then head back down," said the first climber.

His partner dropped to the ground. "I thought you brought the flag," he said.

■ ■ ■

Two elderly sisters donated five dollars to a charity and, to their surprise, won tickets to a football game. Since they had never seen a live football game, Madge thought the free tickets would provide some fun for her and her sister.

"I think so, too," said Mabel. "Let's go!"

They soon found themselves high in a noisy stadium overlooking a large grassy expanse. They watched the kickoff and the seemingly endless back and forth struggles that comprised the scoreless first half.

They enjoyed the band music and cheerleader performance that followed.

Then came the second half. When the teams lined up for the second-half kickoff, Madge nudged her sister. "I guess we can go home now, Mabel," she said. "This is where we came in."

A man on occasion took the Staten Island Ferry. He wasn't too crazy about it, however, because if he missed a ferry late at night, he had to wander the streets of lower Manhattan until the next one arrived.

One evening, he spotted the ferry about fifteen feet from the dock. He didn't want to wait for the next one, so he made a running leap and landed on his hands and knees—a bit bruised, but at least he was safe on deck.

Pulling himself to his feet, he proudly said with a smile, "Well, I made it, didn't I?"

"You sure did," a passenger replied, "but if you had waited for a minute or two, the ferry would have been docked."

■ ■ ■

A tenant placed his order at the pet store: "I need at least fifty mice, two thousand ants, and as many of those little silverfish as you have."

The clerk replied, "We can probably do that, but it's a strange request. Mind if I ask why?" The tenant replied, "I've taken a job in another city, and the landlord told me to leave the apartment the way I found it."

An elderly lady's vision was deteriorating, but she knew she could still see well enough to drive.

One morning, she phoned the police to report that someone had broken into her car. "The dashboard is missing, as well as the steering wheel, the radio, the pedals, and even the glove compartment!" she hollered excitedly.

Within five minutes, a police officer was on his way; but before he arrived, the lady called the police station a second time. "Never mind," she said sheepishly. "I got into the backseat by mistake."

■ ■ ■

A reporter interviewed a 103-year-old woman. "And what is the best thing about being 103?" the reporter asked.

She simply replied, "No peer pressure."

BONUS FUNNY

∎ ∎ ∎

CHILDREN'S BOOKS THAT DIDN'T QUITE MAKE IT:

- You Are Different, and That's Bad
- The Boy Who Died From Eating All His Vegetables
- The Kid's Guide to Hitchhiking
- Whining, Kicking, and Crying to Get Your Way
- Things Rich Kids Have, but You Never Will
- Eggs, Toilet Paper, and Your School
- Why Can't Mr. Fork and Mrs. Electrical Outlet Be Friends?

2. EDUCATIONAL SITUATIONAL

May all who search for you be
filled with joy and gladness.
PSALM 70:4 NLT

How much better it would be if the schooling
I've received as an adult had been part of the
curriculum in the schooling of my youth.
JON LAWHON

— — — — —

Q: Why can you always tell what Dick and Jane
will do next?
A: They're so easy to read.

■ ■ ■

Teacher: The law of gravity explains why we stay on
the ground.
Chloe: How did we stay on the ground before the
law was passed?

■ ■ ■

Q: What's the difference between a cat and a
comma?
A: A cat has its claws at the end of its paws;
a comma is a pause at the end of a clause.

Solid center surrounded by molten layers and a thin crust. The Earth sounds delicious.

■ ■ ■

The college English professor emphasized, over and over again, the importance of developing an extensive vocabulary. "You have my assurance," he told the class, "that if you repeat a word eight or ten times, it will be yours for life."

In the back row, an attractive young woman sighed and, closing her eyes, whispered softly to herself, "Stephen, Stephen, Stephen. . ."

■ ■ ■

A woman was found guilty in traffic court. When asked for her occupation, she said she was a schoolteacher.

The judge spoke from the bench. "Madam, I have waited years for a schoolteacher to appear before this court." He smiled with delight. "Now sit down at that table and write 'I will not run a red light' five hundred times."

■ ■ ■

One day a math teacher and his brother were out golfing. The brother was to tee off first, and just before he swung, he yelled, "Fore!"

The math teacher was up next, and just before he swung, he yelled, "Square root of sixty-four divided by two!"

A kindergarten teacher was showing her class an encyclopedia page illustrating several national flags. She pointed to the American flag and asked, "What flag is this?"

A little girl called out, "That's the flag of our country."

"Very good," the teacher said. "And what's the name of our country?"

The girl answered, " 'Tis of thee."

■ ■ ■

A teacher asked the kindergartners, "Can a bear take off his warm overcoat?"

"No," they answered.

"Why not?"

Finally, after a long silence, a little fellow spoke up. "Because only God knows where the buttons are."

■ ■ ■

Tracy hadn't talked to her grandparents for a while and decided she should call and update them.

"I had a terrible time!" she told them. "First off I got tonsillitis, followed by appendicitis and pneumonia. After that, I got rheumatism, and to top it off they gave me hypodermics and inoculations. I thought I would never get through that spelling bee!"

A son returned home from his freshman year of college. "Great news, Dad!" he exclaimed.

"What's the great news?" his dad asked.

"You don't have to buy me any new books next year. I'm taking all the same courses again."

■ ■ ■

A mother said, "Son, it's time to get up and go to school."

"Mom," her son replied, "nobody at school likes me—the students don't, the teachers don't, the bus drivers don't. . . . I don't want to go to school!"

His mom firmly said, "Son, you must go to school. You are healthy, you have a lot to learn, and you are a leader. . .and besides, you are the principal!"

■ ■ ■

Science teacher: What is the difference between electricity and lightning?
Student: We don't have to pay for lightning.

■ ■ ■

Teacher: Missy, please use the word contrive in a sentence.
Missy: When my brother gets his license, he contrive.

Two college students lost track of time and were late to their math final. Thinking quickly, they smeared some grease on their face and hands and agreed on the excuse they would give. By the time they arrived at the classroom, it was empty.

"We're sorry, Professor Reese," said Greg. "We were on our way here and got a flat tire. When we went to change the tire, we found the tire jack was missing, so we had to call for help. We finally got it changed and got here as soon as we could."

"You can come back on Wednesday and take the test," said the professor.

On Wednesday, the students showed up on time to take the exam. Professor Reese had each young man in a separate room with his test papers. The first question was very simple and was worth ten points. The second question noted that it would be worth ninety points. It read, "Which tire?"

■ ■ ■

Joan and her neighbor were talking about their daughters. Joan said, "My daughter is in law school. She's very bright, you know. Every time we get a letter from her, we have to go to the dictionary."

Her neighbor said, "You are so fortunate. Every time we hear from our daughter, we have to go to the bank."

Ironic that a word like "lackadaisical" takes so much effort to write.

■ ■ ■

Laugh, and the class laughs with you. But you get detention alone.

■ ■ ■

Teacher: What does N-E-W spell?
Student: New.
Teacher: That's correct! Now, what does K-N-E-W spell?
Student: Canoe.

■ ■ ■

If sumthing'z wurth doin it's wurth doin rihgt.

■ ■ ■

Jim: Teacher, would you be mad at somebody for something he didn't do?
Teacher: No, of course not.
Jim: Good. I didn't do my homework.

■ ■ ■

I mistyped the word *problem* today and almost didn't correct it because "porblem" just feels like a better word.

A very intelligent boy was fortunate enough to be receiving more education than his parents had, and his vocabulary far outmatched theirs. One day he came home from school and said, "Mother, may I relate to you a narrative?"

"What's a narrative, Harold?" she asked.

"A narrative, Mother, is a tale."

"Oh, I see," said his mother, nodding, and Harold told her the story. At bedtime as he was about to go upstairs, he said, "Shall I extinguish the light, Mother?"

"What's extinguish?" she asked.

"Extinguish means to put out, Mother," said Harold.

"Oh, okay. Yes, certainly."

The next day the pastor stopped in for a visit, and the family dog began to make a nuisance of himself, as dogs will, by begging for goodies from the table. "Harold," said his mother, trying to impress, "please take that dog by the narrative and extinguish him!"

■ ■ ■

"Just to establish some parameters," said the professor, "Mr. Nelson, what is the opposite of joy?"

"Sadness," said the student.

"And the opposite of depression, Ms. Brady?"

"Elation."

"And you, Mr. Jackson, how about the opposite of woe?"

"I believe that would be giddyap."

Teacher: Correct this sentence: It was me who broke the window.

Joey: It wasn't me who broke the window!

■ ■ ■

Teacher: What is the plural of mouse?

Student: Mice.

Teacher: Good. Now, what's the plural of baby?

Student: Twins!

■ ■ ■

An English professor wrote the following words on the blackboard: "Woman without her man is nothing." He then requested that his students punctuate the sentence correctly.

The men wrote: "Woman, without her man, is nothing."

The women wrote: "Woman! Without her, man is nothing."

■ ■ ■

A man was visiting his alma mater. He paused to admire the newly constructed Shakespeare Hall. "It's marvelous to see a building named for William Shakespeare," he commented to the tour guide.

"Actually," said the guide, "it's named for Stephen Shakespeare. No relation."

"Oh, was Stephen Shakespeare a writer, also?" the visitor asked.

"Well, yes," said his guide. "He wrote the check."

■ ■ ■

A teacher had just discussed magnets with her class. At the close of the lesson, she said, "My name begins with *M* and I pick up things. What am I?"

Julia thought for a moment then answered, "Mom!"

■ ■ ■

One day, while out at recess, two boys noticed that a van began rolling down the parking lot with no one in the driver's seat. They quickly ran to the vehicle, jumped in, and put on the emergency brake.

Seconds later, the door opened, and there was the principal, his face red with anger. "What's going on?" he asked.

"We stopped this van from rolling away," said one of the boys.

The principal, huffing and sweaty, said, "I know. It stalled, and I was pushing it."

■ ■ ■

Teacher: Why are you late?
Carl: Because of the sign.
Teacher: What sign?
Carl: The one that says School Ahead,
    Go Slow.

Teacher: Linda, why are you doing your math
multiplication on the floor?
Linda: You told me to do it without using tables!

■ ■ ■

Teacher: John, how do you spell crocodile?
Jim: K-R-O-K-O-D-A-I-L
Teacher: No, that's wrong.
Jim: Maybe it's wrong, but you asked me how I
spell it!

■ ■ ■

Shortest Books Ever Written. . .
    "1000 Years of French Humor"
    "Cooking Gourmet Dishes with Tofu"
    "Everything Men Know about Women"
    "Career Opportunities for Liberal Arts Majors"

■ ■ ■

Teacher: What is the chemical formula for water?
Stella: H-I-J-K-L-M-N-O!!
Teacher: What are you talking about?
Stella: Yesterday you said it's H to O!

■ ■ ■

Teacher: Wayne, name one important thing we
have today that we didn't have ten years ago.
Wayne: Me!

Teacher: Gary, go to the map and find North America.

Gary: Here it is!

Teacher: Correct. Now class, who discovered America?

Class: Gary!

■ ■ ■

Teacher: Brenda, give me a sentence starting with I.

Brenda: I is . . .

Teacher: No, Brenda. Always say, "I am."

Brenda: All right. . . I am the ninth letter of the alphabet.

■ ■ ■

Teacher: Can anybody give an example of coincidence?

Jerry: My Mother and Father got married on the same day, same time.

■ ■ ■

Teacher: George Washington not only chopped down his father's cherry tree, but also admitted to doing it. Now do you know why his father didn't punish him?

Thomas: Because George still had the ax in his hand.

A wise schoolteacher sends this note to all parents on the first day of school: "If you promise not to believe everything your child says happens at school, I'll promise not to believe everything he says happens at home."

■ ■ ■

Teacher: Now, Steve, tell me frankly, do you say prayers before eating?

Steve: No sir, I don't have to; my Mom is a good cook.

■ ■ ■

Teacher: Darrin, your composition on "My Dog" is exactly the same as your brother's. Did you copy his?

Darrin: No, teacher, it's the same dog!

■ ■ ■

A linguistics professor was lecturing his class one day. "In the English language," he said, "a double negative forms a positive. In other languages, such as Russian, a double negative is still a negative. However, there is no language wherein a double positive can form a negative."

A voice from the back of the room said, "Yeah, right."

Bonus Funny

■ ■ ■

In-Flight Safety

Pilot—"Folks, we have reached our cruising altitude now, so I am going to switch the seat belt sign off. Feel free to move about as you wish, but please stay inside the plane till we land. . . . It's a bit cold outside, and if you walk on the wings, it affects the flight pattern."

■ ■ ■

As the plane landed and was coming to a stop at Washington National, a lone voice comes over the loudspeaker: "Whoa, big fella. WHOA!"

■ ■ ■

"As you exit the plane, please make sure to gather all of your belongings. Anything left behind will be distributed evenly among the flight attendants. Please do not leave children or spouses."

■ ■ ■

From the pilot during his welcome message: "We are pleased to have some of the best flight attendants in the industry. . . . Unfortunately none of them are on this flight."

3. ACTIONS – REACTIONS

A time to cry and a time to laugh.
ECCLESIASTES 3:4 NLT

Just did the math and found out I can retire
next year if I start saving $244,468.02 a month.
JON LAWHON

— — — — —

A woman boarded a plane with her sister. As she passed the pilot, she said, "Now don't start going faster than sound. We haven't seen each other in a long time, and we want to talk."

■ ■ ■

They say there's no excuse for laziness, but I'm going to look for one anyway. On second thought, never mind. Don't feel like putting in the effort.

■ ■ ■

A man was seated on an airplane, preparing for his first flight. As he buckled his seat belt, he turned to the woman seated next to him and asked, "Would you happen to know about how often jetliners like this crash?"

After a brief pause, she answered, "Usually only once."

Sydney: I must have sneezed fifty times today. Do
   you think there's something in the air?
Matt: Yes, your germs!

■ ■ ■

A woman angrily jumped out of her car after
colliding with another car. "Why don't people ever
watch where they're driving?" she hollered. "You're
the third car I've hit today!"

■ ■ ■

Guide: I don't guide hunters anymore, only
   fishermen.
Hunter: Why?
Guide: I have never been mistaken for a fish.

■ ■ ■

"I've had horrible indigestion for the past two
days," a patient said.
   "And what have you been doing for it?" asked
the doctor.
   "Taking an antacid twice a day and drinking
nothing but milk," said the patient.
   "Good—exactly what I would have suggested
myself. That'll be fifty dollars."

■ ■ ■

If it's the thought that counts, from now on I'm
wearing workout pants while I eat.

"Do you believe in life after death?" the boss asked his youngest employee.

"Yes, sir," the young man replied.

"Well, good!" said the boss with a scowl. "Because just after you left early yesterday to go to your grandmother's funeral, she stopped in to see you!"

■ ■ ■

"You must be the worst caddie in the world," said the dejected golfer after a disastrous afternoon on the course.

"I doubt it, sir," replied the caddie. "That would be too much of a coincidence."

■ ■ ■

Exhausted hiker: I am so glad to see you! I've been lost for three days!

Other hiker: Well, don't get too excited. I've been lost for a week.

■ ■ ■

"I see our neighbors have returned our grill," the wife commented. "They've had it for eight months, and I was afraid that in their move, they'd take it with them by mistake."

"That was our grill?" shouted her husband. "I just paid twenty dollars for it at their yard sale!"

First octopus: What do you like least about being
    an octopus?
Second octopus: Washing my hands before dinner.

■ ■ ■

A young businessman had just started his own
firm. He had leased a beautiful office and had it
furnished with antiques. Sitting behind his desk, he
saw a man come into the outer office. Wishing to
appear busy, the businessman picked up the phone
and started to pretend he had a big deal working.
Finally, he hung up and asked the visitor, "May I
help you?"

"Sure," the man said. "I've come to hook up
your phone!"

■ ■ ■

"I think I deserve a raise," the man said to his boss.
"You know there are three other companies after me."

"Is that right?" asked the manager. "What other
companies are after you?"

"The electric company, the phone company,
and the gas company."

■ ■ ■

Karate makes sense. If you practice breaking boards
in half, you'll be able to protect yourself the next
time a board attacks you!

Scientists say space travel makes the skin of astronauts thinner. Apparently half the people in the United States have been astronauts.

■ ■ ■

Mr. and Mrs. Wilson had reached the airport just in time to make their flight. "I wish we'd brought the piano with us," said Mr. Wilson.

"Why on earth would you bring the piano?" asked Mrs. Wilson.

"That's where the tickets are."

■ ■ ■

Patient: Help me, Doc. I can't remember anything
for more than a few minutes. It's driving
me crazy!
Doctor: How long has this been going on?
Patient: How long has what been going on?

■ ■ ■

George came home from a game of golf, and his neighbor asked how he did.

"Oh, I shot seventy," said George.

"That's great!" commended the neighbor.

"Yeah," George said, "and tomorrow I'll play the second hole."

Two barbershops were in red-hot competition. One put up a sign advertising haircuts for seven dollars. His competitor put up one that read, WE REPAIR SEVEN-DOLLAR HAIRCUTS.

■ ■ ■

After weeks of agonizing physical training, the police academy cadets still hadn't been admitted to the firing range.

"I don't get it," huffed one trainee to another as they pounded out yet another five-mile jog.

"What do you mean?"

"We still don't know how to protect people and property, but we're getting real good at running away."

■ ■ ■

Son: Mom, Dad left for work without his glasses, didn't he?
Mom: Yes. How did you know?
Son: The garage door is missing.

■ ■ ■

You mix the ingredients together. You bake it. You slice it into several pieces. You serve each person a piece of it. The leftovers sit in the fridge until somebody wants to revisit it. It gets revisited until there's nothing left but crumbs. And that. . . is *The Life of Pie*!

Tell a man there are three hundred billion stars in the universe, and he believes you. Tell him a bench has wet paint on it, and he has to touch it to be sure.

■ ■ ■

A woman wrote a check at a department store.

"I'll have to ask you to identify yourself," the clerk said.

The customer took a small mirror from her handbag, looked into it keenly, and pronounced, "Yes. That's definitely me."

■ ■ ■

Greg: Do you think there's intelligent life on Mars?
Greta: I sure do. You don't see them spending billions of dollars to come here, do you?

■ ■ ■

Salesman: You make a small down payment, but then you don't make any payments for six months.
Customer: Who told you about me?

■ ■ ■

Ian: My neighbors were screaming and yelling at three o'clock this morning!
Mark: Did they wake you?
Ian: Nah. . .I was already up playing my bagpipes.

The prospective buyer of a home in an exclusive subdivision had to appear before the neighborhood association's screening committee.

"Do you have small children?" was the first question.

"No."

"Outdoor pets?"

"No."

"Do you play any musical instrument at home?"

"No."

"Do you often host personal or business guests who might arrive in more than two vehicles at one time?"

"No." And by now, the prospect had decided the restrictions weren't for him. He held up his hand, rose from his chair, and told the panel, "We may as well call off the deal right now. You need to be aware I sneeze on the average of two or three times a week."

■ ■ ■

The front door of Todd's home was warped, causing the door to jam on occasion. To pry it open, the family kept a hatchet handy.

One day the doorbell rang. Todd peeked out through the curtains and then shouted in a voice that could be heard through the door, "Quick, Kevin, it's the pastor. Get the hatchet!"

Stan: Remember last year when I was broke and
    you helped me, and I said I'd never forget you?
Fred: Yes, I remember.
Stan: Well, I'm broke again.

■ ■ ■

My teenage daughter thinks I'm too nosy. At least
that's what she keeps writing in her diary.

■ ■ ■

Two paramedics loaded the accident victim into the
ambulance.

"I don't understand what happened," the
patient said. "I know I had the right-of-way."

"Yes, you did," replied one of the paramedics.
"But the other driver had the eighteen-wheeler."

■ ■ ■

Tech support: I need you to right-click.
Customer: Okay.
Tech support: Did you get a pop-up menu?
Customer: No.
Tech support: Okay. Right-click again. Do you see
    a pop-up menu now?
Customer: No.
Tech support: Okay, sir. Can you tell me what you
    have done up until this point?
Customer: Sure, you told me to write *click,* and I
    wrote *click.*

Jury duty thoughts: Today I wanted so badly to see the judge use his gavel to crack walnuts.

■ ■ ■

Lawyer to defendant: Do you wish to challenge any of the jury members?
Defendant: Well, I think I could take that guy on the end.

■ ■ ■

On her way back from the concession stand, Marge asked a man at the end of the row, "Excuse me, but did I step on your foot a few minutes ago?"

Expecting an apology, the man said, "Yes, you did."

Marge nodded. "Oh, good. Then this is my row."

■ ■ ■

A man was trying to teach his daughter to drive. Suddenly she screamed, "What do I do now? Here comes a telephone pole!"

■ ■ ■

Al: I caught a twenty-pound salmon last week.
Sal: Were there any witnesses?
Al: There sure were. If there weren't, it would have been forty pounds.

Computer salesperson: This computer will do half
    your work for you.
Customer: Then I'll take two!

■ ■ ■

"Your horse is very well behaved," the lady noted to
the resting rider.

    "Oh, that's true," he replied. "When we come
to a fence, he always stops quickly and lets me go
over first!"

■ ■ ■

A man told his two brothers that he wanted to be
buried at sea along the coast of Maine rather than
in the church cemetery. The brothers both drowned
trying to dig the grave.

■ ■ ■

A man asked the barber, "How much for a haircut?"
    "Twenty dollars," said the barber.
    "And how much for a shave?"
    "Twelve dollars."
    "Okay, then, shave my head."

■ ■ ■

Two fleas were walking out of a theater when they
discovered it was raining hard.
    "Shall we walk?" said one flea.
    "No," said the other. "Let's take a dog."

A computer technician was called to a small business to repair a computer. He wasn't able to find a close parking spot, so he left his car in a no parking zone and placed a note on his windshield saying, "James Bauer, computer technician, working inside the building."

He completed his work within thirty minutes and returned to his car to find a ticket with a note that read, "Peter Westin, police officer, working outside the building."

■ ■ ■

I try to look at the positive side of things. For example, when you're attacked by a cyclops, you only need to use half as much pepper spray.

■ ■ ■

A man whose son had just passed his driving test went home one evening and found that the boy had driven into the living room. "How on earth did you manage to do that?" he fumed.

"Quite simple, Dad. I came in through the kitchen and turned left!"

■ ■ ■

My memory is so bad I can't remember the last time I forgot something.

Two men are talking at work Monday morning.
"What did you do last weekend?"

"Dropped hooks into water."

"Went fishing, huh?"

"No, golfing."

■ ■ ■

As a boy, he had survived the terrible Johnstown, Pennsylvania flood of 1889, and throughout his long life, he told the story to everyone he met.

When he died and went to heaven, he asked Saint Peter if he could tell everyone there the story of the big flood. Peter said it could be arranged.

"But I should warn you," Peter said, "Noah will be in the audience."

■ ■ ■

Two truck drivers came to a low bridge. The clearance sign said, 10 FEET 8 INCHES. When they got out and measured their truck, they discovered their vehicle was eleven feet. The first man looked at the other and said, "I can't see any cops around. Let's go for it!"

■ ■ ■

A football fan is a guy who'll yell at the quarterback for not spotting an open receiver forty-five yards away then head for the parking lot and not be able to find his own car.

Three mice are sitting around boasting about their strengths. The first mouse says, "Mousetraps are nothing! I do push-ups with the bar."

The second mouse pulls a pill from his pocket, swallows it, and says with a grin, "That was rat poison."

The third mouse got up to leave. The first mouse says, "Where do you think you're going?"

"It's time to go home and chase the cat."

■ ■ ■

I've always wondered what *Carpe Diem* means. I think I'll look it up tomorrow.

■ ■ ■

A man telephoned his neighbor at four o'clock in the morning and said, "Your dog is barking and keeping me awake."

The neighbor called him back at 4:00 a.m. the next day and said, "I don't have a dog."

■ ■ ■

A lady aboard a cruise ship was not impressed by the jazz trio in one of the shipboard restaurants. When her waiter came around, she asked, "Will they play anything I ask?"

"Of course, madam."

"Then tell them to go play shuffleboard."

Did you hear about the cowboy who wore paper pants, a paper shirt, paper boots, and a paper hat? The sheriff arrested him for rustling.

■ ■ ■

A fisherman accidentally left his day's catch under the seat of a bus. The next evening's newspaper carried an ad: "If the person who left a bucket of fish on the number forty-seven bus would care to come to the garage, he can have the bus."

■ ■ ■

A man called a lawyer and asked, "How much would you charge for answering three simple questions?"

"Nine hundred dollars," the lawyer replied.

"Nine hundred dollars!" the man exclaimed. "That's a lot, isn't it?"

"Yes, it is," said the lawyer. "Now, what's your third question?"

■ ■ ■

Employer: I thought you requested yesterday afternoon off to go see your dentist.

Employee: Yes, sir.

Employer: Then why did I see you coming out of the stadium with a friend?

Employee: That was my dentist.

A man arrived at the emergency room with both of his ears badly burned. "How did this happen?" the doctor asked.

"I was ironing my shirt when the phone rang, and I answered the iron by mistake," explained the man.

"Well, what about the other ear?" the doctor inquired.

"Oh—that happened when I called for the ambulance."

■ ■ ■

The following was uttered in the monthly departmental meeting: We are going to continue to have meetings every day until we find out why no work is getting done.

■ ■ ■

She: Let me get this straight. The less I hit the ball, the better I am doing.
He: That's right.
She: Then why hit it at all?

■ ■ ■

I see my indecisiveness as a gift. Or a curse.

■ ■ ■

The pirate was wondering why he was no longer getting telephone calls, and then he realized he left it off the hook.

Judge: Have you ever held up a train?

Outlaw: Now and then.

Judge: Where have you held up trains?

Outlaw: Here and there.

Judge: What things have you taken from passengers?

Outlaw: This and that.

Judge: Sheriff, lock this man up!

Outlaw: Hey! When do I get out of jail?

Judge: Oh, sooner or later.

■ ■ ■

Two antennae decided one day to get married. The wedding wasn't that good, but the reception was great!

■ ■ ■

Football is a game where twenty-two big, strong players run around like crazy for four hours while fifty thousand people who really need the exercise sit in the stands and watch them.

■ ■ ■

Boss: Why are you always late getting to work?

Employee: Well, it's been my experience that it helps make the day go by more quickly.

Cleo: Officer, that man is annoying me!

Cop: But he's not even looking at you.

Cleo: That's what's annoying me!

■ ■ ■

Two men went duck hunting with their dogs but were having no success.

"I think I figured out what we're doing wrong," said the first hunter.

"Oh, yeah? What's that?" asked the other.

"We're not throwing the dogs high enough."

■ ■ ■

Sign just before a bridge: WHEN THIS SIGN IS UNDERWATER, THIS ROAD IS IMPASSABLE.

■ ■ ■

Sometimes I half expect my plate of food to speak up and sorrowfully ask why I never take its picture.

Bonus Funny

■ ■ ■

Do you remember when. . .

- Decisions were made by going "eeny-meeny-miney-moe"?
- Mistakes were corrected by simply exclaiming, "Do Over!"?
- Catching the fireflies could happily occupy an entire evening?
- It wasn't odd to have two or three "Best Friends"?
- The worst thing you could catch from the opposite sex was "cooties"?
- Having a weapon in school meant being caught with a slingshot?
- "Oly-oly-oxen-free" made perfect sense?
- Spinning around, getting dizzy, and falling down was cause for giggles?
- The worst embarrassment was being picked last for a team?
- Baseball cards in the spokes transformed any bike into a motorcycle?
- Taking drugs meant orange-flavored chewable aspirin?
- Water balloons were the ultimate weapon?

4. THE STORYTELLER

You will fill me with joy in your presence.
PSALM 16:11 NIV

Went to a food court the other day.
They found me guilty. The crowd went wild,
then the judge yelled out, "Order! Order!"
JON LAWHON

— — — — —

A tourist traveled through the thickest jungles in Central America and came across an ancient Mayan temple. He asked the tour guide for details of the structure. The guide informed him that archaeologists were excavating and still finding great treasures. The tourist then asked how old the temple was.

"This temple is 1,504 years old," replied the guide.

Impressed at this accurate dating, the tourist questioned how there could be such a precise date.

"Oh, that's simple," replied the guide. "The archaeologists said the temple was 1,500 years old, and that was four years ago."

The transatlantic flight to England was halfway across when the pilot came on the intercom with a casual message to the passengers. "You may have noticed a slight change in the sound of the engines. That's because we've had to shut down engine two temporarily. There's no cause for concern; we have three more engines in fine condition. But there'll be a slight delay. Our expected time of arrival has been changed from 2:14 p.m. to 2:45 p.m. Sorry for any inconvenience this may cause."

An hour later the pilot was back on the intercom, chuckling softly. "Folks, this is the first time I've ever experienced this, and I never thought it would happen, but we seem to have lost power in engine four. No problem in terms of safety, but we'll have a further delay. We now expect to arrive at Heathrow International at 3:30 p.m."

And a little while later he was back at the mike, still trying to sound reassuring but with an edge in his voice. "You won't believe this, but engine one seems to be on the brink, and we've decided it's wise to shut it down. This is a weird situation, but not really alarming. We can easily finish the flight with one engine, although we'll be flying substantially slower. We now anticipate arriving around 4:25 p.m."

One passenger turned to another and mumbled, "If that last engine goes out, it'll be next Tuesday till we get to England."

A nervous passenger decided to spring for one of those on-the-spot, low-investment-high-benefits insurance policies at the airport before her plane departed. Then she had time for a quick lunch, so she stopped at a Chinese diner along the terminal walk. Her eyes widened when she read the fortune cookie: "Today's investment will pay big dividends!"

■ ■ ■

Frank and Jerry, two judges, were each arrested on speeding charges. When they arrived in court on the appointed day, no one was there. So instead of wasting time waiting, they decided to try each other. Motioning Frank to the witness stand, Jerry said, "How do you plead?"

"Guilty, Your Honor."

"That'll be fifty dollars and a warning from the court." Jerry stepped down and the judges shook hands and changed places.

"How do you plead?" asked Frank.

"Guilty."

Frank thought for a moment. "These reckless driving cases are becoming all too common," he said. "In fact, this is the second such incident in the last fifteen minutes. That will be three hundred dollars and five days in jail."

Stevie Wonder and Tiger Woods are in a conversation when Tiger turns to Wonder and asks, "How is the singing career going?"

Stevie Wonder replies, "Not too bad! How's the golf?"

Tiger responds, "Not too bad. I've had some problems with my swing, but I think I've solved that problem."

Wonder suggests, "I've always found that when my swing goes wrong, I need to stop playing for a while and not think about it. Then, the next time I play, it seems to be all right."

Surprised, Tiger asks, "You play golf, Stevie?"

Stevie Wonder answers, "Oh, yes. I've been playing for years."

Tiger exclaims, "But you're blind. How can you play golf?"

Wonder replies, "I get my caddie to stand in the middle of the fairway and call to me. I listen for the sound of his voice and play the ball toward him. Then, when I get to the ball, the caddie moves to the green or farther down the fairway, and again I play the ball toward his voice."

"But how do you putt?"

"Well," says Stevie, "I get my caddie to lean down in front of the hole and call to me with his head on the ground, and I just play the ball toward his voice."

Tiger asks, "What's your handicap?"

Stevie answers, "I'm a scratch golfer."

An incredulous Tiger Woods says, "We've got to play a round sometime," and Wonder replies, "Well, people don't take me seriously, so I can only play for serious money, never less than ten thousand dollars a hole."

Woods thinks about it and says, "Okay, I'm game for that. When would you like to play?"

To which Stevie responds, "Pick a night!"

■ ■ ■

A man returns from an overseas trip feeling very ill. He goes to see his doctor and is immediately rushed to the hospital to undergo a barrage of tests.

The man wakes up after the tests in a private room at the hospital. The phone by his bed rings.

"Hello. This is your doctor. We have received the results from your tests. We've found you have an extremely contagious virus."

"Oh, no!" cried the man. "What are you going to do?"

"Well," said the doctor, "we're going to put you on a diet of pizzas, pancakes, and pita bread."

"And that will cure me?" asked the man.

The doctor replied, "Well, no, but it's the only food we can slide under the door."

One morning a lion woke up determined to show the rest of the animals just who was the boss. Strolling through the jungle, he grabbed a monkey by the tail and pulled it from the tree. "Who's the king of the jungle?" he roared.

"Y–y–you are, oh mighty lion!" the monkey said.

Walking past the mud wallow, the lion spotted a warthog. "Who is the king of the jungle?" he roared.

Sinking down into the mud, the warthog whimpered, "You are, oh mighty lion!"

Jumping in between a giraffe's legs, the lion roared up, "Who is the king of the jungle?"

With its knees knocking, the giraffe squealed, "You are, oh mighty lion!"

Wondering who else was going to be unlucky enough to get in his way, the lion found some elephant tracks. Running up behind it, he jumped onto the startled elephant's back and roared, "Who is the king of the jungle?"

The elephant whipped its trunk back, wrapped it around the lion, and knocked him against several nearby trees before letting him go. Only just managing to stand up and stagger away, the lion shouted back, "Okay, okay! No need to be grumpy just because you don't know the answer!"

One cold winter day, two guys were ice fishing about twenty feet apart. The first guy wasn't having any luck. The second guy was pulling out a fish every time he put his line in the water. This made the first guy curious. "Hey," he yelled to the other, "what are you using for bait?"

The other guy yelled back, "Mphh mphh oggth mfft phrr brrt wmmm."

The first guy was very puzzled and said, "What?"

Again the second guy yelled back, "Mphh mphh oggth mfft phrr brrt wmmm."

Finally the first guy had to know what the other guy was saying, so he got up and walked over to him and said, "I couldn't understand a word. What were you saying?"

The second guy spit something into his hand and replied, "I said, you have to keep your bait warm."

A woman walked into a pet store and told the clerk that she'd like to buy a parrot. "I have three parrots," said the shopkeeper. "They were all owned by members of the elementary school's staff. This first one belonged to a principal."

"Squawk!" said the parrot. "You're expelled!"

The store clerk showed her a second parrot. "This one belonged to the English teacher."

"To be or not to be," said the parrot.

"May I see the third one?" asked the woman.

"That one belonged to a bus driver," explained the clerk.

"And what does he say?" the woman questioned.

"Sit down and be quiet!" squawked the parrot.

■ ■ ■

A cowboy found himself in need of money and decided to sell his horse. The local blacksmith was interested, and as they completed the deal, the cowboy mentioned, "This is not an ordinary horse."

"What do you mean?" the blacksmith asked.

The cowboy explained. "He does not respond to the commands of 'Whoa' or 'Giddyap.' When you want this horse to stop, you must say, 'Amen.' When you want him to go, you must say, 'Praise the Lord!' "

Later that day, the blacksmith took the horse out for a ride. Trotting down the road, the horse was startled by a snake and bolted. Soon it was careening full speed toward a cliff. Panicky, the blacksmith shouted "Whoa!" over and over until he remembered the cowboy's instructions. A loud "Amen!" brought the horse to a stop at the edge of the cliff.

Relieved, the blacksmith wiped his brow and exclaimed, "Praise the Lord!"

■ ■ ■

Herb had spent all afternoon interviewing for a new job. He began by filling out all the papers. The human resources manager then questioned him at length about his training and past work experience.

Herb then was given a tour of the plant and was introduced to the people he would be working with.

Finally, he was taken to the general manager's office. The manager rose from his chair, shook his hand, and asked him to sit down. "You seem to be very qualified," he said, "and we would like you to come work for us. We offer a good insurance plan and other benefits. We will pay you six hundred dollars a week starting today, and in three months, we'll raise it to seven hundred dollars a week. When would you like to start?"

"In three months," Herb replied.

A man flying in a hot-air balloon suddenly realizes he's lost. He reduces height and spots a man down below. He lowers the balloon further and shouts to get directions, "Excuse me, can you tell me where I am?"

The man below says: "Yes. You're in a hot-air balloon, hovering thirty feet above this field."

"You must work in Information Technology," says the balloonist.

"I do," replies the man. "How did you know?"

"Well," says the balloonist, "everything you have told me is technically correct, but it's of no use to anyone."

The man below replies, "You must work in management."

"I do," replies the balloonist. "But how'd you know?"

"Well," says the man, "you don't know where you are or where you're going, but you expect me to be able to help. You're in the same position you were before we met, but now it's my fault."

■ ■ ■

A new pastor was asked to perform a funeral for a man that he had never met before. Unable to say anything about the man himself, he asked those present to share.

"Is there anyone here who can say something good about this man?" the pastor asked. There was no response.

"Well, is there someone here who can say something halfway decent about this man?" the pastor asked again. There was nothing but silence from the crowd.

"Is there anyone here who can say anything at all that is at least somewhat positive about this man?" the pastor implored.

Finally, an older gentleman stood up and said, "Well, he wasn't quite as bad as his father!"

■ ■ ■

A traffic cop in a small town stopped a motorist for speeding. "But Officer," said the driver, "I can explain—"

"Save your excuses," said the cop. "You can cool your heels in jail till the chief gets back."

"But Officer. . ."

"Quiet!" snapped the cop. "You're going to jail. The chief will deal with you when he gets back."

A few hours later the officer looks in at the prisoner. "Lucky for you that the chief's at his daughter's wedding. It means he'll be in a good mood when he gets back."

"Don't count on it," said the prisoner. "I'm the groom."

An elderly woman walked to the sanctuary door where a deacon, serving as usher, greeted her.

"Where would you like to sit?" the deacon asked.

"The front row, please," the woman answered.

"You really don't want to do that," the deacon replied. "The pastor is pretty boring."

The woman's eyes narrowed. "Do you know who I am?" she asked.

"No," he said.

"I'm the pastor's mother!" she replied furiously.

"Do you know who I am?" he asked.

"No," she said.

"Good!" he answered and ducked out the door.

A woman is out looking for a pet, and so she's visiting the local pet shops. She walks into a small pet shop and explains her need to the attendant. He thinks for a moment and then says, "I think I have just the thing for you, ma'am. I'll just get him."

With that, he disappears into a back room and returns with a cute little puppy. "This dog is a very special dog," he tells her. "It can fly," he explains, and with that throws the dog into the air. It immediately begins to float gracefully around the shop.

"There is one problem with him, however. Whenever you say 'my,' he will eat whatever you've mentioned. Watch. 'My cookie!' " The lady watches in amazement as the dog zooms over to the shop attendant and devours a cookie he has taken from his pocket.

"He's cute and so extraordinary. I'll take him," she says, and a few minutes later she is on her way back home with the dog to show her husband.

"Sweetheart, look at this amazing pet I bought today!" she exclaims when she gets back home. "He can fly!"

The husband looks at the dog and then says, "Fly, huh? Ha! My foot!"

The following are some allegedly true maintenance problems as submitted by pilots and the solution recorded by maintenance engineers. Never let it be said that ground crews and engineers lack a sense of humor. (P = The problem logged by the pilot. S = The solution and action taken by the engineers.)

P: Left inside main tire almost needs replacement.
S: Almost replaced left inside main tire.

P: Something loose in cockpit.
S: Something tightened in cockpit.

P: Evidence of leak on right main landing gear.
S: Evidence removed.

P: IFF inoperative.
S: IFF always inoperative in OFF mode.

P: Suspected crack in windshield.
S: Suspect you're right.

P: Number three engine missing.
S: Engine found on right wing after brief search.

P: Aircraft handles funny.
S: Aircraft warned to straighten up, fly right, and be serious.

A magazine photographer was assigned to get photos of a forest fire. The smoke at the scene was too thick to get any good pictures, so he called his office to request a plane.

"I'll have it waiting for you at the airport," promised his editor.

He arrived at the airport, and there was the plane near the runway. He jumped into it and yelled, "Let's go!" The pilot took off, and soon they were in the air.

"Fly over to the north side of the fire," said the photographer. "And then make a low-level pass."

"Why?" asked the pilot.

"Because I'm going to take pictures!" the photographer explained, exasperated.

There was a long pause; then the pilot said, "You mean you're not the instructor?"

A couple of friends went hunting for moose in Canada each year. Each time they went, they were flown out to the marshland in a small bush airplane. After they landed at the hunting site, the pilot said, "I'll be back in three days to get you. You can only return with yourselves, your gear, and one moose."

Three days later, the pilot landed to pick them up. The men were standing ready with two moose. "I told you only one moose!" the pilot shouted. "It's impossible to fly out with the weight of two!"

One of the men said, "But last year the pilot took us with two moose, so we thought you could, too."

The pilot, up for the challenge, said, "Well, if he could do it, I can, too."

After they stowed their gear and climbed in, they prepared to take off. The pilot pulled the throttle down as far as it would go. They began to ascend but crashed into a tree at the end of the runway. Moose, gear, and men went in all directions. Lying on the ground, one of the hunters looked around and asked, "Harry, where are we?"

"I'm not sure," answered Harry, "but I'm guessing it's about a hundred yards farther than we made it last year."

An old man rode his bike to his brother's house every Saturday. It took him two hours, and he would always arrive by noon.

One day he wanted to see if he could make it in one hour. But at the top of a hill, he had to stop, suffering from exhaustion. A Corvette pulled up, and the driver asked him if he was in need of a ride. The man glanced at his watch and realized that if he didn't take the driver up on his offer, he would be late. He also saw that there was no room left in the Corvette.

Seeing the man hesitate, the driver said, "It'll be no problem. I have a rope in the back, and we can tie your bike to the back bumper and you can ride. If I go too fast, just yell, 'Beep, beep.'"

They started out and soon came to an intersection. A Ferrari pulled up next to the Corvette, and both vehicles revved their engines. The old man's eyes widened in fear. Sure enough, the light changed, and they were off. The Corvette lost the race, but the guy made it to his brother's house on time.

Meanwhile, at the local police department, one officer said to the others, "The strangest thing just happened. A Ferrari and a Corvette just lost me at over 110 miles per hour on Second Street."

"What's so strange about that?" another officer asked.

The first officer replied, "There was this old man on a bike behind them screaming, 'Beep, beep,' and trying to pass!"

An inexperienced preacher was to hold a graveside burial service at a paupers' cemetery for an indigent man with no family or friends. Not knowing where the cemetery was, he made several wrong turns and got lost.

When he eventually arrived an hour late, the hearse was nowhere in sight, the backhoe was next to the open hole, and the workmen were sitting under a tree eating lunch.

The diligent young pastor went to the open grave and found the vault lid already in place. Feeling that he should conduct the service despite his tardiness, he preached an impassioned and lengthy service, sending the deceased to the great beyond in style.

As he returned to his car, he overheard one of the workmen say to the other, "I've been putting in septic tanks for twenty years, and I ain't never seen anything like that."

A man took his Rottweiler to the vet and said to him, "My dog is cross-eyed. Is there anything you can do for it?"

"Well," said the vet, "let me take a look at him." So he picked up the dog and had a good look at its eyes.

"Well," said the vet, "I'm going to have to put him down."

"Just because he's cross-eyed?" asked the man.

"No," said the vet, "because he's heavy."

■ ■ ■

Reaching the end of a job interview, the human resources worker asked a young engineer who was fresh out of MIT, "What starting salary were you thinking about?"

The engineer said, "In the neighborhood of $125,000 a year, depending on the benefits package."

The interviewer said, "Well, what would you say to a package of five weeks vacation, fourteen paid holidays, full medical and dental, company matching retirement fund to 50% of salary, and a company car leased every two years?"

The engineer sat up straight and said, "Wow! Are you kidding?"

The interviewer replied, "Yeah, but you started it."

A poor bookseller walked through Central Park on his way home each evening. One Monday a masked man jumped from behind a tree. "Give me your money!"

"I have no money. I'm just a poor bookseller. Here's my wallet; see for yourself."

Finding the wallet and the victim's pockets all empty, the bandit grumbled and ran off into the darkening shrubbery.

The next Monday the same bandit accosted the bookseller. "Give me your money!" Again he made off without a dime.

This happened each Monday evening for a month. Finally the bookseller said to him, "Look, you recognize me. You know I'm only a poor bookseller, and I don't carry any money at all. Why do you waste your time and risk getting caught every Monday?"

The robber replied, "I'm still practicing, and you don't seem to mind too much."

■ ■ ■

Two avid fishermen go on a fishing vacation. They rent all the equipment: the reels, the rods, the waders, a rowboat, a car, even a cabin in the woods. They spend a bundle.

The first day they catch nothing. The same thing happens the second day and the third day. This continues until the last day of their vacation, when one of the men catches a fish.

While they're driving home, they're really depressed. One guy turns to the other and moans, "Do you realize that this one lousy fish we caught cost us fifteen hundred dollars?"

The other guy replies, "Wow! Good thing we didn't catch any more!"

■ ■ ■

Fishing season hasn't opened, and an angler who doesn't have a license is attempting to lure a trout when a stranger draws near and asks, "Any luck?"

The fisherman boasts, "Any luck? Why, this is a wonderful spot. I took ten out of this stream yesterday."

"Is that so? By the way, do you know who I am?" asks the stranger.

"Nope."

"Well, meet the new game warden."

"Oh," gulped the fisherman. "Well, do you know who I am?"

"Nope."

"Meet the biggest liar in the state!"

Somewhat skeptical of his son's newfound determination to work out, the father nevertheless took his teenager to the sports equipment store to look at the weight sets.

"Please, Dad," begged the boy, "I promise I'll use them every day."

"I don't know, Justin. It's a big commitment," the father told him.

"I know, Dad," the boy replied.

"They're not cheap, either," the father continued.

"I'll use them, Dad, I promise. You'll see."

Finally won over, the father paid for the equipment, and they headed for the door. From the sidewalk, he heard his son whimper, "What! You mean I have to carry them all the way to the car?"

■ ■ ■

The owner of a large factory decided to make a surprise visit and check up on his staff. As he walked through the plant, he noticed a young man doing nothing but leaning against the wall. He walked up to the young man and said angrily, "How much do you make a week?"

"Three hundred bucks," replied the young man.

Taking out his wallet, the owner counted out three hundred dollars, shoved it into the young man's hands, and said, "Here is a week's pay—now get out and don't come back!"

Turning to one of the supervisors, the owner asked, "Just how long has that lazy kid been working here?"

"He doesn't work here," said the supervisor. "He was just here delivering our pizzas."

■ ■ ■

When Carl went away on vacation, his brother Ben promised to take care of his cat. The next day, Carl called Ben to see how the animal was doing.

"Your cat is dead," said Ben, matter-of-factly.

"Dead?" said the stunned Carl. "Why did you have to tell me like that?"

"How should I have told you?" asked Ben.

"Well," said Carl, "the first time I called, you could have broken it to me gently. You could have said my cat was on the roof, but the fire department was getting her down. The second time I called, you could have told me the cat fell out of the fireman's arms and broke its neck. The third time I called, you could have said that the vet did everything he could, but Fluffy passed away. That way it wouldn't have been so hard on me."

"I'm sorry," said Ben.

"That's all right. By the way, how's Mother?"

"She's up on the roof," said Ben, "but the fire department is getting her down."

Bonus Funny

∎ ∎ ∎

Camping Tips

- Get even with a bear that raided your food bag by kicking his favorite stump apart and eating all the ants.
- A hot rock placed in your sleeping bag will keep your feet warm. A hot enchilada works almost as well, but the cheese sticks between your toes.
- The best backpacks are named for national parks or mountain ranges. Steer clear of those named for landfills.
- When camping, always wear a long-sleeved shirt. It gives you something to wipe your nose on.
- Take this simple test to see if you qualify for solo camping. Shine a flashlight into one ear. If the beam shines out the other ear, do not go into the woods alone.
- A two-man pup tent does not include two men or a pup.
- A potato baked in the coals for one hour makes an excellent side dish. A potato baked in the coals for three hours makes an excellent hockey puck.

5. FOR THOSE WHO *PUNDERSTAND*

A cheerful heart brings a smile to your face.
PROVERBS 15:13 MSG

I've always believed in the old adage, "Never quit until you succeed." Now if I could only remember what it was I was trying to do.
JON LAWHON

— — — — —

Aaron: What do you like about your job at the hot-air balloon company?
Noah: I get a raise every day.

■ ■ ■

I paid more than two thousand dollars to get a cure for my baldness, but I figured it's better to give than to recede.

■ ■ ■

I've reached an age where my hindsight also needs glasses.

■ ■ ■

Bill: Did you tell Stan the new airplane joke?
Phil: Yeah, but I think it went right over his head.

They call him Franklin Gothic because he looks like the type.

■ ■ ■

A mother elephant's heart broke as she looked at her son. He had been chosen last again. With tears in her eyes she said, "No matter what anyone thinks, you're not irrelephant."

■ ■ ■

Doctor: How is the boy who swallowed the quarter?
Nurse: No change yet.

■ ■ ■

Did you hear the one about heaven? It's way over your head.

■ ■ ■

A man went to the doctor with a piece of lettuce hanging out of his ear. "That looks nasty," said the doctor.

"Nasty?" replied the man. "This is just the tip of the iceberg!"

■ ■ ■

Pilot: Do you wanna fly?
Little boy: Yes!
Pilot: Just a minute. I'll catch one for you.

I've never traveled beyond North America. I guess that makes me incontinent.

■ ■ ■

A new nurse listened while the doctor was yelling, "Typhoid! Tetanus! Measles!"

"Why is he doing that?" she asked another nurse.

"Oh, he just likes to call the shots around here," she replied.

■ ■ ■

Have you heard about the man who sat up all night trying to figure out where the sun went when it set? It finally dawned on him.

■ ■ ■

A truckload of brushes has been stolen. The police are combing the area!

■ ■ ■

There was once a man who invented a wooden car. But he never made any money—no one would buy it because it wooden go.

■ ■ ■

In the news: Earlier today, a police vehicle transporting prisoners collided with a cement truck. Officials are now looking for several hardened criminals.

A tour guide was showing a tourist around Washington, DC. The guide pointed out the place where George Washington supposedly threw a dollar across the Potomac River.

"That's impossible," said the tourist. "No one could throw a coin that far!"

"Well, remember," replied the guide. "A dollar went a lot farther in those days."

■ ■ ■

A lot of these yogurt brands today are simply Greek to me.

■ ■ ■

Farmer: Hey, neighbor—you can't take your sheep home that way.
Neighbor: I was just taking a shortcut across your frozen pond. What's wrong with that?
Farmer: Nobody pulls the wool over my ice.

■ ■ ■

If there's one thing I can't stand, then there are probably more of them.

■ ■ ■

Judge: You have been accused of hitting a comedian with your car then dragging him four blocks.
Driver: It was only three blocks, Your Honor.
Judge: That's still carrying a joke too far.

A spokesperson for the US Mint announced that a new fifty-cent piece was being issued to honor two great American patriots. On one side of the coin would be Teddy Roosevelt and on the other side, Nathan Hale.

When asked why two people were going to be on the same coin, the spokesman replied, "Now, when you toss a coin, you can simply call 'Teds' or 'Hales.'"

■ ■ ■

If I ever open an auto repair facility that specializes in brakes, I'm calling it "Whoa Is Me."

■ ■ ■

Did you hear about the crimes over at that house they're renovating? The shower was stalled while the curtains were held up. Apparently the doors were also hung, and I heard the window was framed for it.

■ ■ ■

Kelly: Where can I find the crossword publisher?
Shelly: Go four blocks down and six across.

■ ■ ■

There was a man who had to go to his relative's graveside service at seven o'clock in the morning. He was not happy about it at all. He wasn't a "mourning" person.

An art thief broke into the Louvre and stole some valuable artwork. But despite his careful planning of the crime, the skillful theft, and the evasion of the law, he was captured only three blocks away from the museum, when he ran out of gas.

The police interrogated him then questioned how he could plot the crime but then make such an elementary error. "Well," he began, "I had no Monet to buy Degas to make the van Gogh."

■ ■ ■

Police were called to a daycare where a three-year-old was resisting a rest.

■ ■ ■

Navy jet pilot: This is it! We're flying faster than the
    speed of sound!
Copilot: What?

■ ■ ■

If you're looking for an ark to save two of every animal, I noah guy.

■ ■ ■

Strained my brain thinking about what sort of colander to buy.

Writing with a broken pencil is pointless.

■ ■ ■

I want to buy something on layaway. It sounds relaxing.

■ ■ ■

Counting sheep to fall asleep has never worked for me nor anyone else I know. I think it's a fleece job.

■ ■ ■

I thought I saw a sausage fly past my window, but it turned out to be a seabird. I think it's taking a *tern for the wurst.*

■ ■ ■

Private: Why are you throwing me out of the Marines, sir?
General: Because you are rotten to the Corps, soldier!

■ ■ ■

A fisherman was bragging about a monster of a fish he caught. A friend broke in and chided, "Yeah, I saw a picture of that fish, and he was all of a half pound."

"Yeah," said the proud fisherman. "But after battling for three hours, a fish can lose a lot of weight."

Bonus Funny

∎ ∎ ∎

Newspaper Headlines

- Police Begin Campaign to Run Down Jaywalkers
- Farmer Bill Dies in House
- Squad Helps Dog Bite Victim
- Enraged Cow Injures Farmer with Ax
- Miners Refuse to Work after Death
- Juvenile Court to Try Shooting Defendant
- Stolen Painting Found by Tree
- Two Soviet Ships Collide, One Dies
- Two Sisters Reunited after 18 Years in Checkout Counter
- Killer Sentenced to Die for Second Time in 10 Years
- Cold Wave Linked to Temperatures
- Red Tape Holds Up New Bridge
- Typhoon Rips Through Cemetery; Hundreds Dead
- Man Struck by Lightning Faces Battery Charge

6. STOP ME IF YOU'VE HEAD THIS BEFORE

A cheerful heart is good medicine.
PROVERBS 17:22 NLT

Hi Diddle Diddle. The cat and the fiddle. The cow jumped over the moon. If you've been seeing any of these things, check your medications quite soon.
JON LAWHON

— — — — —

Frank: Did you hear about the guy who was arrested at the zoo for feeding the pigeons?
Harry: No. What's wrong with feeding the pigeons?
Frank: He fed them to the lions.

■ ■ ■

It was mealtime during the flight on the small airline.

"Would you like dinner?" the flight attendant asked the woman.

"What are my choices?" she asked.

"Yes or no," the attendant replied.

Two friends, one an optimist and the other a pessimist, could never quite agree on any topic of discussion. The optimist owned a hunting dog that could walk on water. He had a plan: Take the pessimist and the dog out duck hunting in a boat.

They got out to the middle of the lake, and the optimist brought down a duck. The dog immediately walked out across the water, retrieved the duck, and walked back to the boat. The optimist looked at his friend and said, "What do you think about that?"

The pessimist replied, "That dog can't swim, can he?"

■ ■ ■

A big-city counterfeiter thought the best place to pass off his phony eighteen-dollar bills would be in a small country town. So, he went off in search of one.

When he found a town that he thought might work, the counterfeiter entered a store and handed one of the bogus bills to the cashier. "Can I have change for this, please?" he asked.

The store clerk looked at the eighteen-dollar bill then smiled and replied, "Sure, mister. Would you like two nines or three sixes?"

During a recent Super Bowl, there was another football game of note between big animals and small animals. The big animals were crushing the small animals. At halftime the coach made an impassioned speech to rally the little animals.
At the start of the second half, the big animals had the ball. On the first play, an elephant got stopped for no gain. On the second play, the rhino was stopped for no gain. On the third down, the hippo was thrown for a five-yard loss.

The defense huddled around the coach, who asked excitedly, "Who stopped the elephant?"

"I did," said the centipede.

"Who stopped the rhino?"

"Uh, that was me, too," said the centipede.

"And how about the hippo? Who hit him for a five-yard loss?"

"Well, that was me as well," said the centipede.

"So where were you during the first half?" demanded the coach.

"Well," said the centipede, "I was having my ankles taped."

The factory foreman inspected the shipment of crystal vases ready to leave the plant and approached his new packer. "I see you did what I asked: stamped the top of each box, This Side Up, Handle with Care."

"Yes, sir," the worker replied. "And just to make sure it arrives safely, I stamped it on the bottom, too."

■ ■ ■

After watching a news account of an airline crash, a teenager was asking his mother about the vital "black box" that's so important to accident investigators.

"It contains a complete record of the plane's diagnostics right up to the instant of the crash," she explained.

"Why isn't it destroyed on impact?"

"Because it's encased in a very special alloy material, I'm sure."

"Then why can't they make the whole airplane out of that material?"

■ ■ ■

Max's phone rang in the middle of the night.

"Hello?" he answered.

"Hello," said a voice. "Is this David?"

"No," said Max. "You must have the wrong number."

"Oh, I'm sorry!" said the caller. "I hope I didn't wake you."

"Oh, that's okay," said Max. "I had to get up to answer the phone anyway."

■ ■ ■

A man was hiking on a nature trail when a bear appeared. The bear gave chase, so the man clambered up the nearest tree. But as he was climbing, he slipped and fell at the feet of the beast.

"Lord, please let this be a Christian bear," the man gasped.

And the bear said, "Heavenly Father, I thank You for this food."

■ ■ ■

A Sunday school teacher was using the squirrel as an object lesson on being prepared. "I'm going to describe something," she told the class, "and I want you to raise your hand when you know what it is." The children waited eagerly.

"This thing lives in trees [pause] and eats nuts [pause]." No hands went up.

"It's gray [pause] and has a long bushy tail [pause]." The children looked at each other, but nobody raised a hand.

"And it jumps from branch to branch [pause] and chatters and flips its tail when it's excited [pause]."

Finally one boy tentatively raised his hand. "Well," he said, "I know the answer must be Jesus. . . but it sure sounds like a squirrel to me!"

A secret agent was directed to a posh condominium complex to contact an anonymous source.

"Williams is the name," he was told by his superior. "Hand him this envelope."

Arriving at the complex, he was confused to find four different Williamses occupying adjacent quarters. He decided to try the second condo. When a gentleman answered his knock, the agent spoke the pass code: "The grape arbor is down."

Looking him over, the man shook his head. "I'm Williams the accountant. You might try Williams the spy. Two doors down."

■ ■ ■

A burglar broke into a home and was looking around. He heard a voice say, "Jesus is watching you." Thinking it was just his imagination, he continued his search.

Again the voice said, "Jesus is watching you."

He turned his flashlight around and saw a parrot in a cage. He asked the parrot if he was the one talking, and the parrot said, "Yes."

He asked the parrot what his name was, and the parrot said, "Moses."

The burglar laughed and asked, "What kind of crazy people would name a parrot Moses?"

The parrot replied, "The same kind of people who would name their pit bull Jesus."

An old couple had been married nearly sixty-five years when they were hit by a car and died. They had both been in good health due to the wife's strict diet and exercise program. They went to heaven and were in awe of the mansion that was prepared for them. They had a beautiful gourmet kitchen, an indoor swimming pool, and a master suite complete with a hot tub. The husband asked Saint Peter how much this was all going to cost.

"It's all free," Saint Peter replied. "You're in heaven now!"

They went outside to see the golf course, which was directly behind their mansion. Saint Peter explained they would have golfing privileges every day and their own cart with their names on it.

"What are the greens fees?" the husband asked.

"This is heaven! You play for free, of course," Saint Peter replied.

Next they went to the clubhouse, and they were just in time for the grandiose breakfast buffet complete with sausage quiche and sizzling bacon.

"How much does it cost for the buffet?" asked the husband.

"Don't you get it, dear?" his wife suddenly replied. "We're in heaven, so it must be free!"

"Well, where are all the healthy foods and low-cholesterol eggs?" the husband asked hesitantly.

"In heaven you can eat as much as you like of anything," Saint Peter replied, "and you will never gain weight or get sick. This is heaven!"

"Are you serious?" the husband said and then looked at his wife. "If it weren't for you and all your bran muffins, I could have been here twenty years ago!"

■ ■ ■

A painter was hired to paint the exterior of a church. His practice was to thin the paint so that he could make a larger profit.

As he was painting the church, torrential rain began to fall, and it washed all the paint off. As quickly as the rain began, it ended, and the sun came out. The painter gazed skyward, and a voice from above said, *"Repaint, and go and thin no more."*

■ ■ ■

The farmer's son was returning from the market with a crate of chickens his father had entrusted to him, when all of a sudden the box fell and broke open. Chickens scurried off in different directions, but the boy walked all over the neighborhood, retrieving the birds and returning them to the repaired crate. Hoping he had found them all, the boy returned home.

"Pa, the chickens got loose," the boy told his father reluctantly, "but I managed to find all nine of them."

"You did well, son," the farmer said, "because you left with only six."

Sherlock Holmes and Dr. Watson were on a camping and hiking trip. The first night out they had gone to bed and were lying looking up at the sky. "Watson," Holmes said, "look up. What do you see?"

"Well, I see thousands of stars."

"And what does that mean to you?"

"Well, I guess it means we will have another nice day tomorrow. What does that mean to you, Holmes?"

"To me, it means someone has stolen our tent."

■ ■ ■

A group of university scientists approached a local pastor to tell him that God was no longer needed. "We've created spaceships, supercomputers, almost life itself," the scientists said. "Human knowledge has advanced to the point that God Himself is obsolete."

The pastor listened politely then said, "I'd like some proof of that. Can you create a human being, like God did with Adam?"

"Sure!" the scientists replied. They invited the pastor to their labs.

At the university, one group of scientists invited the pastor to join them as they prepared an operating table for the big moment. Soon, the other group appeared, carrying buckets of dirt from which to make a man.

"Hey, wait a minute," the pastor said. "That's God's dirt. . .go make your own!"

An old man who raised chickens happened across a mysterious box in his closet. The box contained three eggs and eight hundred dollars. Amazed, he called his wife to ask her about his find.

Embarrassed, she admitted to having hidden the box their entire forty-five years of marriage. Curious, the man asked, "Why would you hide this from me?"

"Oh, I never meant to hurt your feelings," his wife replied.

"What do you mean, hurt my feelings? How could this box hurt my feelings?"

"Well," she responded, "every time I got angry with you, I put an egg in the box."

The man thought that in forty-five years, three times was nothing to feel too bad about, so he asked her what the money was for.

His wife replied, "Every time I got a dozen eggs, I sold them for one dollar."

■ ■ ■

Little Johnny was racing around the neighborhood on his new bike and called out to his mother to watch his tricks:

"Look, Mom, no feet!"

"Look, Mom, no hands!"

"Waaah! Look, Mom, no teeth!"

One afternoon, a woman was in the backyard hanging laundry when an old, tired-looking dog wandered into the yard. She could tell from his collar and well-fed stomach that he had an owner. But when she walked into the house, he followed her, sauntered down the hall, and fell asleep in a corner. Almost an hour later, he went to the door, and she let him out. The next day he was back. He resumed his position in the hallway and slept for an hour. This continued for a couple of weeks. Curious, the woman pinned a note to his collar: "Every afternoon your dog has been coming to my house and taking a nap."

The next day he arrived with a different note pinned to his collar: "Duke lives in a home with six children—he's trying to catch up on his sleep."

■ ■ ■

The fire department was called to the scene of a large fire. One truck arrived well ahead of the others, with the driver speeding through the streets. He quickly doused the flames.

At a dinner given in the fireman's honor, the mayor gave a speech about how he had saved the building, as well as those around it, by getting there so fast and extinguishing the fire.

"What can we give you to show our gratitude for your work?" asked the mayor.

"Brakes," replied the fireman.

At a preacher's convention a pastor got up and started his sermon with this sentence: "I spent the best years of my life in the arms of a woman not my wife." As the congregation gasped, he quickly said, "She was my mother!" The congregation chuckled, and a young preacher tucked it into his memory to use with his own congregation.

Back home he began to feel a bit uncertain that he remembered it right. Forging ahead anyway, he started with, "I spent the best years of my life in the arms of a woman not my wife." The congregation gasped, and the preacher paused, forgetting the punch line. After a few nervous moments he stammered, "And I can't remember who she was!"

■ ■ ■

A man was lying on the grass and looking up at the sky. As he watched the clouds drift by, he asked, "God, how long is a million years?"

God answered, *"To Me, a million years is as a minute."*

The man asked, "God, how much is a million dollars?"

God answered, *"To Me, a million dollars is as a penny."*

The man then asked, "God, can I have a penny?"

God answered, *"In a minute."*

A middle-aged man went to the doctor for his annual checkup. His wife went along. After the man's physical, the doctor called the wife into his office alone.

"Your husband seems to have a very high anxiety level, and it isn't good for his heart," the doctor told her. "If you don't do the following, your husband will surely die."

The doctor then handed her this list:

1. Every morning, fix him a fresh, healthy breakfast.

2. Be kind to him all day and do everything to keep his stress level to a minimum.

3. For lunch, make him a nutritious meal.

4. For dinner, prepare him whatever meal he might desire.

5. Keep the house as peaceful as possible and allow him to rest as much as he wants.

6. Don't allow him to do any chores or anything that might cause undue stress.

On their way out of the doctor's office, the husband asked his wife what the doctor said to her.

"I'm afraid you're going to die," she replied.

An old man had been a faithful Christian and was in the hospital, near death. The family called their pastor to stand with them.

As the pastor stood next to the bed, the old man's condition appeared to deteriorate rapidly, and he motioned frantically for something to write on. The pastor lovingly handed him a pen and a piece of paper, and the man used every ounce of strength to scribble a note before he died. The pastor thought it best not to look at the note at that time, so he placed it in his jacket pocket.

At the funeral, as he was finishing the message, he realized that he was wearing the same jacket that he had been wearing when the man died. He said, "You know, he handed me a note just before he died. I haven't looked at it, but knowing him, I'm sure there's a word of inspiration there for us all."

He opened the note and turned pale as he read aloud the words, "You're standing on my oxygen tube!"

■ ■ ■

A small child on an ocean liner fell overboard. Before his mother could scream for help, a man quickly flew over the rail into the water and saved the child. The hero was pulled back onto the deck and was surrounded by cheering passengers. The captain said, "That was amazing! What can we do to thank you for rescuing the boy?"

"Well," said the man, "you can start by telling me who pushed me overboard!"

■ ■ ■

A man was driving down a quiet country road when a rooster darted in his path.

Whack! The rooster disappeared under the car.

The man saw a cloud of feathers. Shaken, the man pulled over at the farmhouse and rang the doorbell. The farmer appeared. The driver nervously said, "I think I killed your rooster. Please allow me to replace him."

"Suit yourself," the farmer replied. "You can go join the other chickens around back."

■ ■ ■

A young woman went to her doctor, complaining of pain. "Where are you hurting?" asked the doctor.

"I hurt all over," said the woman.

"What do you mean, all over?" asked the doctor. "Be a little more specific."

The woman touched her right knee with her index finger and yelled, "Ow, that hurts." Then she touched her left cheek and again yelled, "Ouch! That hurts, too." Then she touched her right earlobe. "Ow, even that hurts!" she cried.

The doctor examined her for a moment then reported his diagnosis. "Ma'am, you have a broken finger."

A wealthy man was dying, and the thought of leaving behind his money—the fruits of hard life-long work—saddened him. So he began praying to ask if he could take his money with him to heaven.

One night, an angel appeared to the man. "I'm sorry, but the rule is that nobody brings anything to heaven with them. Your money will have to stay behind."

But the man was accustomed to getting his way in business, so he kept up his praying, increasing the urgency of his requests. After a while, the angel reappeared with a new message: "God has heard your prayers and will let you bring one suitcase with you."

The man was thrilled and pulled out the largest piece of luggage he had. Then he filled it with gold bars and coins. Shortly thereafter, he died.

At the gates of heaven, the man appeared with his big suitcase. Saint Peter stopped him, saying, "Wait a minute—you can't bring that in here!" But the man explained the special permission allowed by God and delivered by the angel.

"Well, okay," Peter said. "But I think I should check the contents first."

Peter laid the suitcase on its side and popped open the lid. He stared in amazement for a moment and then exclaimed, "Pavement? You brought pavement to heaven?"

Four men were in the hospital waiting room because their wives were having babies. A nurse went up to the first man and said, "Congratulations! You're the father of twins."

"That's odd," the man replied. "I work for the Minnesota Twins!"

A short time later, the nurse returned and said to the next man, "Congratulations! You're the father of triplets!"

"That's amazing!" answered the man. "I work for the 3M Company!"

Moments later the nurse came out to tell yet another man, "Congratulations! You're the father of quadruplets!"

"Incredible!" he said. "I work for the Four Seasons Hotel!"

The last man looked as if he was going to pass out. "What's wrong?" the others asked.

"I work for 7-Eleven!"

■ ■ ■

A site foreman had ten very lazy men working for him, so one day he decided to trick them into doing some work for a change.

"I have a really easy job today for the laziest one among you," he announced. "Will the laziest man please raise his hand."

Nine hands shot up.

"Why didn't you put your hand up?" he asked the tenth man.

"It was too much trouble."

A university professor, vacationing in the country, struck up a conversation with a local. When the prof learned his acquaintance was a country preacher, he asked the man, "Do you honestly believe that Jonah spent three days and three nights in the belly of a huge fish?"

The preacher responded, "I don't know, sir. But when I get to heaven, I'll ask him."

"But just suppose he isn't there?" the professor pressed.

"Then you ask him."

■ ■ ■

A young executive was preparing to leave the office late one evening when he found the CEO standing in front of a shredder with a piece of paper in his hand.

"This is a very sensitive and important document," said the CEO, "and my secretary has gone for the night. Can you get this thing to work for me?"

"Certainly," said the young executive eagerly. He turned the machine on, inserted the paper, and pressed the Start button.

"Excellent! Thank you!" said the CEO as his paper disappeared inside the machine. "I just need one copy. . . ."

Two guys are in a car. The driver comes to a stoplight and goes right through it. His friend says, "What are you doing?"

The driver says, "It's okay; my brother does it all the time."

They come up to another stoplight and go right through. His friend says, "You are out of your mind."

The driver says, "It's okay; my brother does it all the time."

They come up to a green light, and he stops. His friend says, "It's green—go."

The driver replies, "Oh, no, I can't. My brother might be coming!"

■ ■ ■

A salesman dropped in to see a business customer. No one was in the office. However, he did find a big dog emptying wastebaskets. The salesman stared at the animal, wondering if his imagination could be playing tricks on him.

The dog looked up and said, "Don't be surprised. This is just part of my job."

"Incredible!" exclaimed the man. "I can't believe it. Does your boss know how incredible you are? An animal that can talk!"

"Oh, no," pleaded the dog. "Please don't say anything! If he finds out I can talk, he'll make me answer the phone, too."

A young woman who worked as a clerk in a large company boasted to her friend, "Every day the president of the company speaks to me."

"Really?" asked her friend. "What does he say?"

"He says, 'Will you please quit parking in my parking spot?'"

■ ■ ■

After a long illness, a woman died and went to heaven. While she was waiting for Saint Peter to greet her, she peeked through the pearly gates.

When Saint Peter came by, the woman said to him, "This is such a wonderful place. How do I enter?"

"You have to spell a word," Saint Peter told her.

"Which word?" the woman asked.

"Love."

The woman correctly spelled "L-O-V-E," and Saint Peter gladly welcomed her into heaven.

About a year later, Saint Peter came to the woman and asked her to watch the gates of heaven for him that day.

While the woman was guarding the gates, her husband arrived. "I'm surprised to see you," the woman said. "How have you been?"

"Oh, I've been doing pretty well since you died," her husband told her. "I married the beautiful young nurse who took care of you while you were ill. And then I won the lottery. I sold the little house you and I lived in and bought a big mansion. And my wife and I traveled all around the world. While we were on vacation, I went waterskiing. I fell, the ski hit my head, and I drowned. Here I am now. What do I have to do to get in?"

"You have to spell a word," the woman told him.

"Which word?" her husband asked.

"Czechoslovakia."

■ ■ ■

A man found employment with road maintenance, painting the yellow lines in the middle of the road. On the third day, his supervisor called the worker into his office. "The first day, you painted three miles of highway, the second day one mile, and today you only painted one hundred yards. Why do you keep slowing down?"

The man answered, "I'm doing the best I can. I just keep getting farther away from the can!"

Bonus Funny

■ ■ ■

Murphy's Law Amendments

1. You can go anywhere you want if you look serious and carry a clipboard.
2. Eat one live toad first thing in the morning and nothing worse will happen to you the rest of the day.
3. If at first you don't succeed, try again. Then quit.
4. Mother said there would be days like this, but she never said there would be so many.
5. Important letters that contain no errors will develop errors in the mail.
6. If you are good, you will be assigned all the work.
7. If it wasn't for the last minute, nothing would get done.
8. When you don't know what to do, walk fast and look worried.
9. You will always get the greatest recognition for the job you least like.
10. Machines that have broken down will work perfectly when the repairman arrives.

7. RIDDLED WITH QUESTIONS

But the fruit of the Spirit is. . joy.
GALATIANS 5:22 NIV

Why do some people look surprised in their selfies?
Didn't they know their hand had grabbed their phone?
JON LAWHON

— — — — —

Q: Where did the baseball player keep his mitt?
A: In the glove compartment.

■ ■ ■

Q: What looks just like half an apple?
A: The other half.

■ ■ ■

Q: Who is bigger—Mr. Bigger or Mr. Bigger's baby?
A: Mr. Bigger's baby is a little Bigger.

■ ■ ■

Q: Who wrote *How to Run a Successful Service Station*?
A: Philip McCarr and Bud Aaron D. Tyre.

■ ■ ■

Q: What do you call an airplane that flies
    backward?
A: A receding airline.

Q: Why was the baby ant confused?
A: Because all his uncles were ants.

■ ■ ■

Q: What goes up and down but doesn't move?
A: A staircase.

■ ■ ■

Q: What did the mother buffalo say to her boy as he was leaving?
A: "Bison."

■ ■ ■

Q: Who wrote *The Long Walk Home*?
A: Miss D. Buss.

■ ■ ■

Q: What do you call a moose after a long shower?
A: Bull Wrinkle.

■ ■ ■

Q: What part of a ship is made out of cards?
A: The deck.

■ ■ ■

Q: Why do mountain climbers rope themselves together?
A: To keep the smart ones from quitting.

Q: Which is heavier, a pound of feathers or a pound of bricks?
A: Neither. Both groups weigh exactly one pound.

■ ■ ■

Q: What is over your head and under your hat?
A: Your hair.

■ ■ ■

Q: What dangerous animal did Mrs. Washer have in her backyard?
A: A clothes lion.

■ ■ ■

Q: Which way did the programmer go?
A: He went data way.

■ ■ ■

Q: Why don't matches play baseball?
A: One strike and they're out.

■ ■ ■

Q: Why did the weasel cross the road twice?
A: He was a double-crosser.

■ ■ ■

Q: Why is the law of gravity untrustworthy?
A: It will always let you down.

Q: Who wrote *The New Shoes*?
A: Ben Down and Tye Laces.

■ ■ ■

Q: Where was the Declaration of Independence signed?
A: At the bottom.

■ ■ ■

Q: What did the teddy bear say when he was offered dessert?
A: "No thanks, I'm stuffed."

■ ■ ■

Q: What do you get when you cross an automobile and an eel?
A: I don't know, but every time the battery dies, it recharges itself.

■ ■ ■

Q: What do you get if you cross a cow and an octopus?
A: A cow that can milk itself.

■ ■ ■

Q: Who can jump higher than a house?
A: Anyone. A house can't jump.

Q: What big cat should you never play a card game with?

A: A cheetah.

■ ■ ■

Q: Why doesn't a bike stand up by itself?

A: Because it's two tired.

■ ■ ■

Q: How do baby birds learn to fly?

A: They wing it.

■ ■ ■

Q: Why did the astronaut keep changing his course?

A: He didn't take the time to plan-et!

■ ■ ■

Q: Who wrote Grand Canyon Mishap?

A: Eileen Dover and Phil Lin.

■ ■ ■

Q: What do you get when you cross a dog with an elephant?

A: A very nervous postman.

■ ■ ■

Q: What do babies and basketball players have in common?

A: They both dribble.

Q: What happened to the cow that survived an earthquake?

A: She became a milkshake.

■ ■ ■

Q: What does a thousand-pound canary say?

A: "Here, kitty, kitty, kitty."

■ ■ ■

Q: What is worse than a giraffe with a sore neck?

A: A centipede with athlete's foot.

■ ■ ■

Q: What did the astronaut think of the takeoff?

A: She thought it was a blast.

■ ■ ■

Q: What did the monkey say when its tail was cut off?

A: "Won't be long now."

■ ■ ■

Q: What's the first sign that a computer is getting old?

A: It has memory problems.

■ ■ ■

Q: How do you make a puppy disappear?

A: Use Spot remover.

Q: What did one wall say to the other?
A: "Meet me in the corner."

■ ■ ■

Q: What is another name for a bunch of bees?
A: A good report card.

■ ■ ■

Q: What do you call a man who works in a garden?
A: Bud.

■ ■ ■

Q: What do you call a grizzly bear with no teeth?
A: A gummy bear.

■ ■ ■

Q: What do you get if you cross a cactus and a bicycle?
A: Flat tires.

■ ■ ■

Q: Why do bakers work so hard?
A: Because they need the dough.

■ ■ ■

Q: What is the favorite mode of transportation for accountants?
A: Taxis.

Q: What do you call a sick alligator?
A: An ill-igator.

■ ■ ■

Q: What are goose bumps for?
A: To keep geese from speeding.

■ ■ ■

Q: What did the mommy broom say to the baby broom?
A: "It is time to go to sweep."

■ ■ ■

Q: Why couldn't the coffee bean go out to play?
A: He was grounded.

■ ■ ■

Q: Where do birds invest their money?
A: In the stork market.

■ ■ ■

Q: Who wrote I Love School?
A: I. M. Kidding.

■ ■ ■

Q: What kind of bee is always dropping the football?
A: A fumble-bee.

Q: What did the first arithmetic book say to the other arithmetic book?
A: "I really have a lot of problems."

■ ■ ■

Q: Why did the FBI agent spray his room with Raid?
A: He thought it might be bugged.

■ ■ ■

Q: What ten-letter word starts with G-A-S?
A: Automobile.

■ ■ ■

Q: What do you call a sleeping bull?
A: A bulldozer.

■ ■ ■

Q: Where do you find Timbuktu?
A: Between Timbuk-one and Timbuk-three.

■ ■ ■

Q: If a gardener has a green thumb and bankers have gold thumbs, who has a black-and-blue thumb?
A: A carpenter.

Q: What do you call two banana peels?
A: A pair of slippers.

■ ■ ■

Q: What do you get when you cross a pig and a
centipede?
A: Bacon and legs.

■ ■ ■

Q: What do you call a cat that gets thrown in the
dryer and is never found again?
A: Socks.

■ ■ ■

Q: Who wrote Bifocals and the Men Who Wear
Them?
A: I.C. Clearly.

■ ■ ■

Q: Why won't baseball players form a union?
A: They like to avoid strikes.

■ ■ ■

Q: What did the baby corn say to the mommy
corn?
A: "Where is Pop-corn?"

Bonus Funny

■ ■ ■

A Glossary of Fishing Terms:

- hook: (1) A curved, pointy device used to catch fish (2) A clever advertisement to entice a fisherman to spend his life savings on a new rod and reel (3) The punch administered by a fisherman's wife after he spends their life savings on a rod and reel (see also right hook and left hook).
- line: Something you give your coworkers when they ask how your fishing went the past weekend.
- lure: A device that is only semi-enticing to fish but will drive a fisherman into such a frenzy that he will max out his credit card before exiting the tackle shop.
- reel: A rather heavy object that causes a rod to sink quickly when dropped overboard.
- rod: A scientifically designed length of fiberglass that prevents a fisherman from getting too close to the fish.
- school: A grouping in which fish are taught to avoid $29.99 lures and hold out for cornflakes with peanut butter instead.
- tackle: What your fishing partner did to you as you pulled in the catch of the day.

8. DOWN ON THE FARM

This is the day the LORD has made.
We will rejoice and be glad in it.
PSALM 118:24 NLT

Southern vocabulary lesson. Summers: a word
describing an uncertain location. "I put my
car keys summers an' now I caint find 'em."
JON LAWHON

— — — — —

If baby pigs are called piglets, why aren't baby bulls
called bullets and baby chickens chicklets?

■ ■ ■

Farmer: Quite a storm we had last night.
Neighbor: Yep, it sure was.
Farmer: Did it damage your barn any?
Neighbor: I dunno. I haven't found it yet.

■ ■ ■

A mother mouse and a baby mouse were walking
along when all of a sudden, a cat attacked them.
The mother mouse yelled, "Woof!" and the cat ran
away.
"See?" said the mother mouse to her baby.
"Now do you see why it's important to learn a
foreign language?"

A tourist was on an excursion through the swamps of Florida. "Is it true," he asked the guide, "that an alligator won't attack you as long as you're carrying a flashlight?"

"That depends," replied the guide, "on how fast you carry the flashlight."

■ ■ ■

In West Virginia's rugged coal country, an old preacher told a boy, "Son, remember that faith can move mountains."

"Yeah," the boy replied, "but dynamite's more exciting!"

■ ■ ■

An old Christian cowboy once told his great-grandson his secret to living a long life: "Sprinkle a pinch of gunpowder on your cereal every morning."

One hundred years later, the grandson finally died, having taken his great-grandfather's advice. He left behind ten children, thirty-five grandchildren, sixty great-grandchildren, thirteen great-great-grandchildren, and an eighty-foot hole where the crematory used to be.

■ ■ ■

City slicker, to farmer: Lived here all your life?
Farmer: Not yet.

A lady went to an auto parts store and asked for a seven-ten cap. All the clerks looked at each other, and one said, "What's a seven-ten cap?"

She said, "You know, it's right on the engine. Mine got lost somehow, and I need a new one."

"What kind of a car is it on?" the clerk asked.

"My 2000 Toyota," she replied.

"Well, how big is it?"

She made a circle with her hands about three and a half inches in diameter.

The clerk asked, "What does it do?"

"I don't know, but it's always been there."

At this point, the manager came over. He handed her a notepad and asked her if she could draw a picture of it. The customer carefully drew a circle about three and a half inches in diameter. In the center she wrote, "710."

The manager, looking at the drawing upside down, walked to a shelf and grabbed an *oil* cap.

■ ■ ■

Hunter #1: We're lost. Shoot three shots in the air.
Hunter #2: Okay.
Hunter #1: If no one comes soon, go ahead and shoot three more.
Hunter #2: I hope someone comes soon. We're getting low on arrows.

A small rural town hadn't seen rain for weeks. The crops were dying, the fields were brown, and the people's spirits were anxious.

When weeks turned to months, the community's three churches called a joint meeting on the town square to pray for rain. The pastors asked the townspeople to bring an object of faith to help inspire the prayers.

On the appointed day, everyone showed up to ask God for rain, and the pastors were deeply moved to see the many inspirational objects that were brought along: Bibles, crosses, candles, flowers. But the prayer meeting really got going when a young boy showed up with an umbrella!

■ ■ ■

Tony was having trouble getting his neighbor to keep his chickens fenced in. The neighbor kept talking about chickens being great creatures, and as such, they had the right to go wherever they wanted.

On his next trip to the grocery store, Tony bought a dozen eggs. That night, he snuck out and placed the eggs throughout his yard.

The next morning, when he was sure the neighbor was watching, Tony went out and gathered the eggs. After that, he never had problems again with finding his neighbor's chickens in his yard.

Four men were boasting of the merits of their favorite four-legged friend.

"My ol' Penny goes to the store for me," said one. "She always brings me back my evening newspaper."

"My dog Lacey buys our grits at that same store," said another. "I give her a ten-dollar bill, and she brings me back the change first then returns for the bag of grits."

"I send ol' Pogo there for my shotgun shells," said the third. "He knows exactly what gauge and brand I want".

The fourth man said nothing until he was challenged by the others to try to top their tales. "I reckon my dog ain't much to speak of, by comparison," he answered. "He just sits in the store all day and runs the cash register."

■ ■ ■

A man was riding down a country road. When he rounded a turn, he saw a large group of people outside a house. He stopped and asked a bystander why so many people were there. A man replied, "Jim's mule kicked his mother-in-law, and she died."

"Well," replied the traveler, "she sure had a lot of friends."

"Naw," said the other man, "we're all just interested in buying his mule."

When the usher came by and noticed this, he whispered to the cowboy, "Sorry, sir, but you're only allowed one seat." The cowboy groaned but didn't budge.

The usher became more impatient. "Sir, if you don't get up from there, I'm going to have to call the manager." The cowboy just groaned.

The usher marched briskly back up the aisle. In a moment, he returned with the manager. Together the two of them tried repeatedly to move the cowboy, but with no success. Finally, they summoned the police.

The cop surveyed the situation briefly then asked, "All right Buddy, what's your name?"

"Sam," the cowboy moaned.

"Where ya from, Sam?"

With pain in his voice, Sam whispered. . . "The balcony."

■ ■ ■

Back in the 1800s the Tates Watch Company of Massachusetts wanted to expand their product line, and since they already made the cases for pocket watches, they decided to market compasses for the pioneers traveling west. Although their watches were of the finest quality, their compasses were so bad that people were continually getting lost. This, of course, is the origin of the expression, "He who has a Tates is lost!"

For ten dollars, visitors to the country fair could ride in a barnstormer's biplane. An aging farm couple who'd never traveled outside the county thought they might like to take the opportunity to fly, just for fun. But they were more than a little afraid.

"Tell you what," the barnstormer offered, perceiving their nervousness. "You can ride together, and I'll charge you only five dollars. Just promise me you won't scream or try to tell me how to fly my plane."

They accepted his offer and proceeded with the thrill of their lives. Through a wild series of loops and rolls, the pilot never heard a sound from his backseat companions.

"Wow, Pop, you were just great!" shouted the pilot over his shoulder as he landed the plane. "I thought for sure you'd both holler when we made that nosedive."

"That wasn't so bad," yelled the farmer. "But I almost did break my promise a few minutes before that, when my wife fell out of the airplane."

■ ■ ■

Rancher: What kind of saddle do you want? One with or without a horn?
City slicker: Without is fine. There doesn't seem to be much traffic around here.

A countryman was visiting the city for the first time. Unfortunately, he was accosted by a robber who stuck a gun in his back.

"One move and you're dead," the bad guy growled. "I'm looking for your money."

"Yeah, me, too," the man responded.

■ ■ ■

A farmer had a large patch of watermelons that he was planning to sell in just a few weeks. As he walked through the patch, he discovered that someone had been sneaking in and stealing watermelons.

After some thought, he came up with an idea he felt sure would scare the burglar away. The farmer made a sign reading, WARNING! ONE OF THESE WATERMELONS HAS BEEN INJECTED WITH RAT POISON! and posted it in the field. Pleased with himself, he went to bed.

The next day, the farmer surveyed his field and found that no watermelons were missing. But there was a sign next to his, reading, NOW THERE ARE TWO!

■ ■ ■

Farmer's son: Pa doesn't know whether to get a cow or a tractor.
Cousin: He'd sure look funny trying to ride a cow. . . .
Farmer's son: He'd look even funnier trying to milk a tractor!

At the funeral for a middle-aged farmer, the new country preacher talked at length of the good traits of the departed. The preacher told of what a hard worker and an honest man he was. He also said the farmer was a loving husband and a kind father.

The farmer's widow could take it no more. She leaned over and whispered to one of her sons, "Will you go up there and look in that casket? See if that's your pa."

■ ■ ■

A man ran up to a farmhouse and pounded on the door. When the farmer came to the door, the man demanded, "Where's the nearest train station, and what time is the next train to the city?"

The farmer replied, "You may cut through my field, and you should reach the station in time for the 5:20. But if my bull sees you, you'll probably make it by 5:00."

■ ■ ■

A motorist got his car stuck in the mud while on a drive through the country. A farmer happened to be by the side of the road and offered to pull him out for twenty dollars.

"At that price, I would think you'd be busy day and night, pulling people out," said the motorist.

"Oh, I can't at night," said the farmer. "That's when I haul water for this hole."

A family who lived deep in the woods had no electricity in their home. The wife was about to have her first child, so the father hurried to find a doctor.

At nightfall, the doctor asked the man to bring the lantern. After their baby girl was delivered, the man put the lantern back on the table. Suddenly the doctor said, "Hurry, bring the lantern back," and the man complied.

Another baby girl was delivered, and the man returned the lantern to the table. "Quick," said the doctor. "Bring the light back."

"Doc," said the man, "you don't think they're attracted to the light, do you?"

■ ■ ■

Two cows are standing in a wide-open field. One cow says to the other cow, "Hey, are you worried about that mad cow disease?"

The second cow says, "Why would I be worried about mad cow disease? I'm an airplane!"

■ ■ ■

A preacher was enjoying a meal at the farmhouse of one of his members.

"Your chicken is delicious!" the pastor commented. "How did you prepare it?"

"I didn't do anything special," replied the farmer's wife. "I just told it straight out that it was going to die."

Farmer Brown: Did you lose much in that last tornado?

Farmer Jones: Lost the henhouse and all the chickens. But that was all right—I ended up with three new cows and somebody's pickup truck.

■ ■ ■

A man from out of town drove his car into a ditch on an old country road. A farmer saw his predicament and led his horse to the stranded car. "This is Buddy," he said. He hitched Buddy to the bumper and yelled, "Pull, Lightning, pull!" Buddy didn't move.

Then the farmer hollered, "Pull, Starlight, pull!" Buddy remained still.

He then instructed, "Pull, Nellie, pull!" Buddy still didn't move.

The farmer finally said, "Pull, Buddy, pull!" The horse moved forward and easily pulled the car out of the ditch.

The driver, very thankful, was more than a little curious. He asked the farmer why he called the horse by the wrong name three times.

The farmer explained, "Well, Buddy is blind, and if he knew he was the only one pulling, he wouldn't try at all!"

Upon entering a little country store, a stranger noticed a sign reading: DANGER! BEWARE OF DOG, posted on the glass door.

Inside, he noticed a harmless old hound dog asleep on the floor beside the counter. He asked the store owner, "Is that the dog folks are supposed to beware of?"

"Yup, sure is," he replied.

The stranger couldn't help but smile in amusement. "That certainly doesn't appear to be a dangerous dog to me. Why did you post that sign?"

"Well," the owner replied, "before I posted that sign, people kept tripping over him."

■ ■ ■

A man was driving past a farm and saw a three-legged chicken running alongside his car. Suddenly, the chicken picked up speed and disappeared around the bend. The driver pulled to the side of the road and called to the farmer, "I just saw a three-legged chicken!"

"Oh, yes," said the farmer. "We have a bunch of 'em. We have three people in our family, and we all like drumsticks."

"Well, how do they taste?" asked the motorist.

"Dunno," said the farmer. "We can't catch any."

City slicker: I finally went for a ride this morning.
Ranch hand: Horseback?
City slicker: Yep, he got back about an hour before
    I did.

■ ■ ■

A farmer loaded a cow into a truck to transport it
to another barn. A couple of miles down the road,
he lost control of the truck. It ran off the road and
overturned in the ditch by the side of the road.

When the police officer arrived, he first found
the cow, suffering with two broken legs. He went
ahead and put the animal out of its misery.

Circling the vehicle, the officer found the
farmer, lying on the ground. With the gun still in
his hand, he asked the farmer, "Are you okay?"

The man jumped to his feet and quickly said,
"There's nothing wrong with me, Officer!"

Bonus Funny

■ ■ ■

Things Dads Never Say

- Well, how 'bout that? I'm lost! Looks like we'll have to stop and ask for directions.
- You know Pumpkin, now that you're thirteen, you'll be ready for unchaperoned car dates. Won't that be fun?
- I noticed that all your friends have a certain hostile attitude. I like that.
- Here's a credit card and the keys to my new car. GO CRAZY!!
- Your Mother and I are going away for the weekend. You might want to consider throwing a party.
- Well, I don't know what's wrong with your car. Probably one of those doo-hickey thingies–ya know–that makes it run or something. Just have it towed to a mechanic and pay whatever he asks.
- No son of mine is going to live under this roof without an earring. Now quit your bellyaching, and let's go to the mall.
- Whaddya wanna go and get a job for? I make plenty of money for you to spend.
- What do I want for my birthday? Aahh– don't worry about that. It's no big deal.

9. KID SPEAK

Rejoice in the Lord always.
PHILIPPIANS 4:4 NKJV

I totally take back all those times when
I was younger and didn't want to nap.
JON LAWHON

— — — — —

A little girl asked her mother for fifty cents to give to an old lady in the park. Her mother was touched by the child's kindness and gave her the required sum.

"There you are," said the mother. "But tell me, isn't the lady able to work anymore?"

"Oh yes," came the reply. "She sells candy."

■ ■ ■

Girl: Grandma, were you on Noah's ark?
Grandma: Of course not, dear!
Girl: Then how did you survive the flood?

■ ■ ■

"Jenny!" called her mother, "Why are you feeding birdseed to the cat?"

"I have to," Jenny replied. "That's where my canary is."

A man holding a football leaned over his garden gate and shouted to two boys on the other side of the street, "Is this your ball?"

"Did it do any damage, mister?"

"No, it didn't."

"Then it's ours," said the boy.

■ ■ ■

After church one Sunday, a young boy walked up to the pastor. "Pastor," he said, "I heard you say in church that our bodies came from the dust."

"That's right, son, I did."

"And didn't you say that when we die, our bodies go back to dust?"

"Yes, I'm glad you were listening," the pastor replied. "Why do you ask?"

"Well I think you better come over to our house right away and look under my bed," the boy said, " 'cause there's someone either coming or going!"

■ ■ ■

A group of kindergartners was on a class outing to their local police station where they saw pictures, tacked to a bulletin board, of the ten most-wanted men.

One of the youngsters pointed to a picture and asked if it really was the photo of a wanted person.

"Yes," answered the policeman.

"Well," wondered the child, "why didn't you keep him when you took his picture?"

A father was showing pictures of his wedding day to his son. "Is that when Mommy came to work for us?" the boy asked.

■ ■ ■

Sunday school teacher: Why did Moses wander in the desert for forty years?
Ginny: Because he was too stubborn to stop and ask for directions?

■ ■ ■

One evening as a mother was preparing dinner, her seven-year-old son came down to the kitchen, crying hysterically. The loving mother bent down and said, "Honey, what's wrong?"

"Mom," he said, "I just cleaned my room."

"Well, I'm very proud of you," she replied. "But why on earth would that make you cry?"

Her son looked up through his tears and said, "Because I still can't find my snake!"

■ ■ ■

One day a father was driving with his five-year-old daughter, when he honked his car horn by mistake. "I did that by accident," he said.

"I know that, Daddy," she replied.

"How did you know that?"

"Because you didn't holler at the other driver after you honked it."

A mother, much against her better judgment, finally gave in and bought the children a dog with the understanding that they would care for it. They named the dog Laddy. It wasn't long before the responsibility fell to the mother, and she found that she was taking care of the dog all by herself. Since the children did not live up to their promise, she decided to sell Laddy.

One of the kids sorrowfully said, "We'll miss him."

Another said, "If he wouldn't eat so much and wouldn't be so messy, could we please keep him?"

Mom stood strong and held her ground. "It's time to take Laddy to his new home."

"Laddy?" the children asked. "We thought you said Daddy."

■ ■ ■

At the beginning of math class, the teacher asked, "Ty, what are 3 and 6 and 27 and 45?"

Ty quickly answered, "NBC, CBS, ESPN, and the Cartoon Network!"

■ ■ ■

"Tell me," the teacher asked her students, "do you know what the word *can't* is short for?"

"Yes," said little Lucy. "It's short for cannot."

"Very good. And what about don't?"

Little Matt's hand shot up. "That," he said with authority, "is short for doughnut."

The students in a second-grade class were asking their teacher about her newly pierced ears.

"Does the hole go all the way through?"

"Yes."

"Did it hurt?"

"Just a little."

"Did they use a needle?"

"No, they used a special gun."

Silence followed, and then one solemn voice quietly asked, "How far away did they stand?"

■ ■ ■

"I've never seen a hand so filthy," Mother said to Sammy when he came in from playing.

"Then take a look at this one," said Sammy, holding up his other hand.

■ ■ ■

Dear God, I didn't think orange went with purple until I saw the sunset You made on Tuesday. That was cool!

■ ■ ■

"Hey, you!" yelled the ranger to the small child. "Can't you read that sign? No fishing in this river!"

"I'm not fishing!" came the perky reply. "I'm teaching my worm how to swim!"

The mother was furious. "Ricky," she called to her son, "last night when I turned out the kitchen light and went to bed, there were four Twinkie packages in the cookie jar. This morning there are only two. What do you know about this?"

"Well, it was kinda dark," Ricky confessed. "I only saw two packages."

■ ■ ■

A boy sat on the side of the road with his fishing line down in a drain. Feeling sorry for him and wanting to humor him, a lady gave him fifty cents and kindly asked, "How many have you caught?"

"You're the tenth this morning," was the reply.

■ ■ ■

Little Amy confided to her uncle, "When I grow up, I'm going to marry the boy next door."

"Why is that?"

"Cause I'm not allowed to cross the road."

■ ■ ■

Some Boy Scouts from the city were on a camping trip. The mosquitoes were so fierce, the boys had to hide under their blankets to avoid being bitten. Then one of the Scouts saw some lightning bugs and said to his friend, "We might as well give up. They're coming after us with flashlights."

Dad: What happened to your eye?
Keith: I was staring at a ball from afar, and I was wondering why it was getting bigger and bigger. Then, it hit me.

■ ■ ■

A little boy took the chair at the barbershop.

"How would you like your hair cut today, son?" asked the barber.

"Oh, do it like you do Daddy's, with the big hole at the back."

■ ■ ■

An exasperated mother, whose son was always getting into trouble, asked him, "How do you expect to get into heaven?"

The young boy thought for a minute and said, "Well, I'll just keep slamming the front door and running in and out until Saint Peter says, 'For heaven's sake, come in or stay out!' "

■ ■ ■

Police officer: Where are you going?
Child: Running away.
Police officer: I've been watching you for ten minutes, and you keep walking around the block.
Child: But I'm not allowed to cross the street by myself.

A little boy showed his father a ten-dollar bill he had found in the street.

"Are you sure it was lost?" asked his father.

"Yes," answered the boy. "I saw the man looking for it."

■ ■ ■

A three-year-old had been told several times to get ready for bed. The last time his mom told him, she was very insistent. His response was, "Yes, sir!"

Correcting him, she said, "You would say, 'Yes, sir,' to a man. I am a lady, and you would say 'Yes, ma'am,' to a lady."

To quiz him on this lesson, she then asked him, "What would you say to Daddy?"

"Yes, sir!" came the reply.

"Then what would you say to Mama?"

"Yes, ma'am!" he proudly answered.

"Good job! Now, what would you say to Grandma?"

He lit up and said, "Can I have a cookie?"

■ ■ ■

"Dad, is it okay to eat bugs?" the son asked.

"We shouldn't talk about bugs while we're eating," his father answered.

Later that evening, his father asked, "What did you want to ask me about at dinner?"

"Never mind now," his son answered. "There was a bug in your potatoes, but it's gone now."

"Does anyone remember anything we learned about Solomon?" a Sunday school teacher asked.

"He had three hundred wives and seven hundred porcupines," a little boy answered.

■ ■ ■

A family was having a fun day at the beach when the youngest child happened to notice a dead seagull lying in the sand. Heartbroken over the situation, the young child ran to her mommy and asked, "What could have happened to him?"

Not sure what to say, her mother hesitated and then said, "He died and went to heaven, honey."

This seemed to please the young girl for a moment, but then she asked, "Did God throw him back down?"

■ ■ ■

A family was driving past a fire station, and a discussion broke out among the kids after they saw the Dalmatian sitting out front. "They use him to keep crowds back," said one of the children.

"No," argued another child. "He's just for good luck."

"No," disagreed the oldest child. "They use him to find the fire hydrants."

Mother had just finished waxing the floors when she heard her young son opening the front door. She shouted, "Be careful on that floor, Jimmy; it's just been waxed!"

Jimmy, walking right in, replied, "Don't worry, Mom, I'm wearing my cleats."

■ ■ ■

A mother was driving with her young son to a funeral for a distant relative. Since the five-year-old boy had never been to a funeral, the mother took the time to explain what would happen at the service and what happens to people when they die.

At the grave site, the mother realized that her explanation hadn't been as thorough as she thought when her son leaned over and, in a voice loud enough for all to hear, asked, "Mom? What's in the box?"

■ ■ ■

On the way to preschool, the doctor let his daughter look at his stethoscope. The little girl picked it up and began playing with it. This thrilled the father as he thought, *Perhaps one day she will follow in my footsteps and become a doctor.*

But then he heard her as she spoke into the instrument, "Welcome to McDonald's. May I take your order?"

A boy was visiting the zoo with his father. They were at the tiger display, and the boy's dad was explaining about how dangerous they can be.

"Daddy, if the tigers escaped and ate you—"

"Yes?" his father asked.

"How would I get home?"

■ ■ ■

A mother saw her young son come through the door with filthy hands. She stopped him and said, "My goodness, what would you say if I came in the house with hands like that?"

Her son looked at her and answered, "I think I'd be too polite to mention it."

■ ■ ■

A young boy and his friends were filling in a hole in his backyard when his neighbor happened to see them.

"What are you doing, boys?" his neighbor asked.

"We're having a funeral for my goldfish," replied the boy with a sob. "He just died, and we buried him."

"That's a really big hole for just a little goldfish!" the neighbor said, looking at the large mound of dirt.

"That's because he's inside your cat!" said the boy.

A little boy bought a box of soap flakes, telling the clerk he needed to wash his dog. The clerk told him to be very careful because it was a strong detergent.

The next time the boy came in, the clerk asked him about his dog, and the boy said, "He died."

"Well, I told you that I thought it would be too strong to wash a little dog," the clerk said.

"I don't think it was that," the boy explained. "I think it was the rinse cycle that got him."

■ ■ ■

A young child walked up to her mother and stared at her hair. As her mother scrubbed on the dishes, the girl cleared her throat and asked, "Why do you have some gray hairs?"

The mother paused and looked at her daughter. "Every time you disobey, I get a strand of gray hair."

The mother returned to her task of washing dishes. The little girl stood there thinking. She cleared her throat again. "Mom?" she said.

"Yes?" her mother answered.

"Why is Grandma's hair all gray?"

A minister was visiting the home of a family in his congregation. Their little son ran in, holding a mouse by the tail.

"Don't worry, Mom, it's dead," he reported. "We chased him, then hit him until. . ."

Just then he caught sight of the minister. He lowered his voice and eyes and finished, ". . .until God called him home."

■ ■ ■

Son: I'll be good for twenty dollars.
Dad: Well, when I was your age, I was good for nothing.

Bonus Funny

■ ■ ■

How to Annoy Your Man on Super Bowl Sunday:

- Take the batteries out of all the remote controls.
- Show a sudden interest in every aspect of the game. Especially have him define the offside rule many times.
- Decide it's time to dust the house, starting with a particularly good dusting of the television set right at kickoff.
- Invite your mother over for the game.
- Get a magazine, sit in the room, and read extra good passages aloud.
- Invite your friends over for any sell–from–home party.
- It's your night out with the girls; leave the kids home with him!

10. LOVE AND MARRIAGE

Let your wife be a fountain of blessing for you.
Rejoice in the wife of your youth.
PROVERBS 5:18 NLT

The most effective way to remember
your wife's birthday is to forget it once.

— — — — —

A husband was watching a baseball game on television when his wife said, "Speaking of high and outside, the grass needs mowing."

■ ■ ■

An employee went to see his supervisor. "Boss," he said, "we're doing some heavy housecleaning at home tomorrow, and my wife asked me to help with the attic and the garage, moving and hauling stuff."

"We're shorthanded," the boss replied. "I can't give you the day off."

"Thank you," said the employee. "I knew I could count on you!"

■ ■ ■

Husband: Hey, Marie, do you have anything you want to say before the football season starts?

A man was constantly telling his wife that he thought he could do a better job of keeping the house clean. So she handed the responsibilities over to him.

The first evening that he took on the challenge, his wife returned home to discover that her husband had baked a cake, frosted it, cleaned the counters and the surfaces of all the appliances, scrubbed the kitchen floor, walls, and ceiling, and even had time to shower.

She burst into tears because she felt inadequate. She just couldn't get that much accomplished in such a short amount of time.

He took her in his arms and gave her a hug, admitting that while he was making the frosting, the mixer popped out of the bowl and the beaters threw frosting all over the kitchen, requiring that he clean everything before she returned.

■ ■ ■

Wife: Should we really be taking the car out in this rainstorm?
Husband: Sure. It's a driving rain, isn't it?

■ ■ ■

Marriage is an institution where two people come together to jointly solve the problems they never had before they got married.

Grandpa John was celebrating his 100th birthday and everybody complimented him on how athletic and well preserved he appeared. "Gentlemen, I will tell you the secret of my success," he cackled. "I have been in the open air day after day for some seventy-five years now."

The celebrants were impressed and asked how he managed to keep up his rigorous fitness regime.

"Well, you see my wife and I were married seventy-five years ago. On our wedding night, we made a solemn pledge. Whenever we had a fight, the one who was proved wrong would go outside and take a walk."

■ ■ ■

"Cash, check, or charge?" I asked after folding items the woman wished to purchase. As she fumbled for her wallet, I notice a remote control for a television set in her purse.

"Do you always carry your TV remote?" I asked.

"No," she replied. "But my husband refused to come shopping with me, so I figured this was the most annoying thing I could do to him."

■ ■ ■

Husband: The bank returned your check.
Wife: Good, now I can use it for something else.

A couple was vacationing at a northern fishing resort. Husband Bill liked to fish at the crack of dawn. Angie, his wife, preferred to read. One morning Bill returned after several hours on the lake and decided to take a short nap.

Angie decided to take the boat out. She was not familiar with the lake, but she rowed out to a nice spot and resumed reading her book. In a few minutes the sheriff putted up alongside and greeted her. "Good morning, ma'am. May I ask what you're doing?"

"Why, I'm reading my book, Officer."

"You're in a restricted fishing area."

"But sir, I'm not fishing. Can't you see that?"

"But you have all the equipment, ma'am. I'll have to take you in and write you up."

"If you do that I will charge you with armed harassment."

"I didn't even draw my gun," groused the sheriff.

"Yes, that's true," Angie responded, pointing to the sheriff's holster. "But you have all the equipment."

■ ■ ■

Wife: Do you love me just because my father left me a fortune?

Husband: Not at all, darling. I would love you no matter who left you the money.

An elderly couple was on a road trip. The wife, who couldn't hear very well, was doing the driving.

They stopped for gas, and a man at another gas pump said, "That is the nicest car I've ever seen. What kind is it?" The husband told him it was a Mercedes.

"What did he say?" shouted the wife. The husband told her that the man just wanted to know what kind of car they drove.

The man at the pump asked, "Where are you folks from?" The husband told him they were from Dallas, Texas.

"What did he say?" called the wife.

"He wanted to know where we are from," reported the husband.

The man at the pump said, "That's where I met a woman a few years back. She was the meanest woman I have ever met!"

"What did he say?" hollered the wife.

"He said he thinks he knows your sister," the husband said.

■ ■ ■

A man and his wife attended a dinner party at the home of their friends. Near the end of the meal, the wife reprimanded her husband. "That's the third time you've gone for dessert," she scolded. "The hostess must think you're an absolute pig."

"I don't think so," he said. "I've been telling her it's for you."

Kim said to her friend, "I just don't understand the attraction golf holds for men."

"I know!" Rachel responded. "I went golfing with Roger one time, and he told me I asked too many questions."

"I'm sure you were just trying to understand the game. What questions did you ask?"

"Oh, just things like, 'Why did you hit the ball into that lake?' "

■ ■ ■

Tired of having to balance his wife Dot's checkbook, Dave made a deal with her: he would only look at it after she had spent a few hours trying to get it into shape. Only then would he lend his expertise.

The following night, after spending hours poring over the figures, Dot said, "There! I did it! I made it balance!"

Dave was impressed and came over to take a look. "Let's see. . .mortgage, eight hundred dollars; electricity, ninety-seven dollars and twelve cents; telephone, forty-eight dollars and seventy-three cents. . ." His brow wrinkled as he read the last entry. "It says here ESP, six hundred and forty-four dollars. What is that?"

"Oh," she said, "that means 'Error Some Place.' "

A doctor's receptionist answered the phone and was screamed at by an excited man at the other end of the line.

"My wife's in labor!" he yelled. "I think she's going to deliver any minute now."

"Please calm down," the receptionist said. "Try to relax and give me some basic information. Is this her first child?"

"No, no! I'm her husband!"

■ ■ ■

An elderly man bought a cell phone and decided to try it out. As he was driving on the freeway on his way home, he called his wife. "Hey, sweetheart," he said. "I'm on the freeway!"

"Please be careful," his wife said worriedly. "I just heard on the radio that there's a crazy driver driving the wrong way."

"*A* crazy driver?" he exclaimed. "No. . .there's hundreds of them!"

■ ■ ■

Wife: You don't look well. What's the matter?
Husband: You know those aptitude tests we give
    our employees?
Wife: Yes.
Husband: Well, I took one today, and it's a good
    thing I own the company.

"You just go ahead," said the man to his wife when they got to the mall. "While you're shopping, I'll just look around in the hardware store."

An hour later, she returned and saw him at the checkout counter. The clerk was ringing up the last of a pile of tools and supplies that would fill the car.

"Are you buying all this?" his wife asked him in surprise.

"Well, yes," he said. "But look at all the stuff I'm leaving behind."

■ ■ ■

An elderly man, knowing he was at the end of his life, was in bed at his home just waiting for death to claim him.

His wife was in the kitchen baking cookies. He could smell the delicious aroma of his favorite cookies and decided that he wanted one last cookie before he died.

His wife was unable to hear his quiet, raspy voice as he called out for a cookie, so he mustered up enough strength to climb into his wheelchair and wheel out into the kitchen. He lifted his thin arm to the cookie sheet and grabbed hold of a large, warm chocolate-chip cookie.

Just then his wife gently whacked his hand with her spatula. "What was that for?" he gasped.

"Those are for the funeral," she replied.

A husband, proving to his wife that women talk more than men, showed her a study that indicated that men use on the average only fifteen thousand words a day, whereas women use thirty thousand words a day. "Well," she replied, "that's because women have to repeat everything they say when they're talking to men."

"What?" he asked.

■ ■ ■

A man asked his wife, "What would you most like for your birthday?"

She said, "Oh, I'd love to be ten again."

He came up with a plan, and, on the morning of her birthday, he took her to a theme park. They rode every ride in the park together.

Lunchtime soon came, so into a fast-food restaurant they went, where she was given a large cheeseburger, with french fries and a milkshake.

After lunch, he took her to a movie theater to watch the latest movie for kids—complete with popcorn and soda.

At last she staggered home with her husband and collapsed into bed. Her husband leaned over and asked, "So, sweetheart, what was it like being ten again?"

She looked at him and said quietly, "Actually, I meant the dress size."

Employee: My wife says I should ask you for a raise.

Employer: I'll ask my wife if I can give you one.

■ ■ ■

His marriage in trouble, a man decided to attend church. There, he asked the pastor if they could discuss his marital issues privately.

In a counseling room, the pastor asked several questions to gauge the man's situation then suggested the man take his wife a gift to show his love.

The visitor shook his head. "What can you give a wife who has everything, yet none of it is paid for?"

■ ■ ■

A man and wife rushed into a dentist's office. The wife said, "I want a tooth pulled. I don't want any gas or numbing agent because I'm in a terrible hurry. Just pull the tooth as quickly as possible."

"You certainly are a brave woman," said the dentist. "Now, show me which tooth it is."

The wife turned to her husband and said, "Open your mouth and show the dentist which tooth it is, dear."

■ ■ ■

Husband: What do you mean our financial
     situation is fluid?

Wife: We're going down the drain.

An old man was afraid that his wife was losing her hearing. So he walked up close to her and asked, "Can you hear me?"

She didn't answer.

He walked up closer and asked again. But there was no answer.

Finally he asked her one more time, really loudly, and his wife said, "For the third time, yes!"

■ ■ ■

A couple was going out for the evening to celebrate their anniversary. While they were getting ready, the husband put the cat outside. The taxi arrived, and as the couple walked out the door, the cat shot back into the house.

Not wanting their pet to have free run of the house while they were out, the husband went back upstairs to get the cat.

The wife didn't want it known that there would be no one home, so she said to the taxi driver, "My husband will be right back. He's just going upstairs to say good-bye to his mother."

A few minutes later, the husband climbed into the car and said, "I'm sorry I took so long. The old thing was hiding under the bed, so I had to poke her with a coat hanger to get her to come out!"

One morning a woman said to her husband, "I bet you don't know what day this is."

"Of course I do," he indignantly answered, going out the door on his way to the office.

At eleven o'clock, the doorbell rang, and when the woman answered it, she was handed a box containing a dozen long-stemmed red roses.

At one o'clock, a foil-wrapped box of her favorite chocolates arrived.

Later in the afternoon, a boutique delivered a designer dress.

The woman couldn't wait for her husband to come home. "First the flowers, then the candy, and then the dress!" she exclaimed when he walked in the door. "I've never had a more wonderful Groundhog Day in my whole life!"

■ ■ ■

Wife: You're so involved with golf that you can't remember the day we were married.
Husband: That's what you think. It was the same day I sank a thirty-five-foot putt.

A husband raced into his house. "I've found a great job!" he exclaimed to his wife. "The pay is incredible, they offer free medical insurance, and give three weeks' vacation!"

"That does sound wonderful," said the wife.

"I'm glad you think so," replied her husband. "You start tomorrow."

■ ■ ■

A wife went fishing with her husband. After several hours, she remarked, "I haven't had this much fun since the last time I cleaned the oven."

BONUS FUNNY

■ ■ ■

CLASSIFIED ADS

- Washer $100. Owned by clean bachelor who seldom washed.
- Free puppies. . .part German shepherd-part dog.
- Free Yorkshire terrier. 8 years old. Unpleasant little dog.
- German shepherd 85 lbs. Neutered. Speaks German. Free.
- Free 1 can of pork & beans with purchase of 3 br 2 bath home.
- Bill's septic cleaning "we haul American-made products."
- Shakespeare's pizza-free chopsticks.
- Hummels-largest selection ever "if it's in stock, we have it!"
- Georgia peaches-California grown-89 cents lb.
- Nice parachute: never opened-used once-slightly stained.
- Free: farm kittens. Ready to eat.
- Ground beast: 99 cents lb.
- Fully cooked boneless smoked man-$2.09 lb.

11. FUNNY SHORTS

My spirit rejoices in God.
LUKE 1:47 NIV

Sometimes I take certain rocks for granite.
JON LAWHON

— — — — —

Our team was so bad that when they played the National Anthem, the flag was at half-staff.

■ ■ ■

My cat is so smart. He eats cheese then waits at the mouse hole with baited breath.

■ ■ ■

Eggs and ham: A day's work for a chicken, a lifetime commitment for a pig.

■ ■ ■

Parachute recall notice: On page 12 of instruction manual, please replace "state ZIP code" with "Pull rip cord."

■ ■ ■

A cookbook is being compiled. Please submit your favorite recipe and a short antidote for it.

Heard about the guy who had to quit his job due to illness and fatigue? His boss was sick and tired of him.

■ ■ ■

Jake: Our town's baseball league is the worst!
Jack: How bad is it?
Jake: It's so bad the kids throw away the baseball cards and collect the bubble gum.

■ ■ ■

Make life more interesting. In that moment when you're about to sneeze, stand up and make it the first part of an interpretive dance.

■ ■ ■

Plan ahead—it wasn't raining when Noah built the ark.

■ ■ ■

Sign in front of a house: ANYONE IS WELCOME TO USE OUR LAWN MOWER, BUT PLEASE DON'T TAKE IT OUT OF OUR YARD.

■ ■ ■

Have you heard the story about the peacock that crossed the road? It really is a colorful tale. . . .

A study of economics usually reveals that the best time to buy anything is last year.

■ ■ ■

A man writing to the meteorologist: I thought you may be interested in knowing that I shoveled eighteen inches of "partly cloudy" from my sidewalk this morning.

■ ■ ■

Misers are no fun to live with, but they make great ancestors.

■ ■ ■

Since I learned to laugh at myself, I'm cracking up just about nonstop.

■ ■ ■

Did you hear about the guy who won a gold medal in the Olympics? He had it bronzed.

■ ■ ■

Hockey players have been complaining about violence for years. It's just that without their teeth, no one can understand them.

■ ■ ■

Sign by the side of the road: DRIVE RIGHT SO MORE PEOPLE WILL BE LEFT.

The geology student needed to find a tutor when his grades went below C level.

■ ■ ■

To a kid with a hammer, everything in life is a nail.

■ ■ ■

Never let your worries get the best of you. Always remember: Moses started out as a basket case!

■ ■ ■

Among the things that money can't buy, is what it used to.

■ ■ ■

It is always unlucky to be behind at the end of the game.

■ ■ ■

Television is called a medium because it's neither rare nor well done.

■ ■ ■

Low Self-Esteem Support Group will meet Wednesday at 6:00 p.m. Please use the back door.

■ ■ ■

Money talks, but it has a one-word vocabulary: good-bye.

The trouble with being a good sport is that you have to lose to prove it.

■ ■ ■

Gained several hundred followers earlier this evening. A swarm of sand gnats followed me from the car to the door.

■ ■ ■

Geologists are really down to earth!

■ ■ ■

A pest control man came to my door. I told him to bug off.

■ ■ ■

The Christmas season is in full swing. I just heard "My Fleas Love Me Not" on the radio.

■ ■ ■

It is truly said that children brighten a home—they never turn off the lights.

■ ■ ■

Hear about the new Windows error message? THREE THINGS IN LIFE ARE GUARANTEED: DEATH, TAXES, AND COMPUTER CRASHES. GUESS WHICH ONE JUST HAPPENED.

Ever wonder what's going on in your eye's blind spot?

■ ■ ■

The safest way to double your money is to fold it once and put it back in your wallet.

■ ■ ■

After four karate lessons, I can now break a two-inch board with my cast.

■ ■ ■

I wish my life had CliffsNotes because the plot is awfully confusing.

■ ■ ■

"What? Where?"—an owl taking it to the next level.

■ ■ ■

On a plumbers truck: "We repair what your husband fixed."

■ ■ ■

Skiing: a winter sport that people learn in several sittings.

■ ■ ■

On the trucks of a local plumbing company: "Don't sleep with a drip. Call your plumber."

Did you hear about the calendar thief? He got twelve months; they say his days are numbered.

■ ■ ■

Pizza shop slogan: "7 days without pizza makes one weak."

■ ■ ■

Bowling is a sport that should be right down your alley.

■ ■ ■

At a towing company: "We don't charge an arm and a leg. We want tows."

■ ■ ■

In a nonsmoking area: "If we see smoke, we will assume you are on fire and take appropriate action."

■ ■ ■

On a maternity room door: "Push. Push. *Push*."

■ ■ ■

At an optometrist's office: "If you don't see what you're looking for, you've come to the right place."

■ ■ ■

Sign at the foot of a ski run: LAWS OF GRAVITY STRICTLY ENFORCED.

If you wear glasses, here's a good tip: Watch two minutes of TV with your glasses off. Then put them on – INSTANT ULTRA HIGH DEF!

■ ■ ■

On a taxidermist's window: "We really know our stuff."

■ ■ ■

Four out of five dental patients surveyed recommend breath mints for their dentists.

■ ■ ■

In a podiatrist's office: "Time wounds all heels."

■ ■ ■

I hate it when people put me on the spot. Don't you?

■ ■ ■

On a fence: "Salesmen welcome! Dog food is expensive."

■ ■ ■

Necessity is the mother of invention—even though much of what's invented is hardly necessary.

At the electric company: "We would be de-lighted if you send in your bill. However, if you don't, you will be."

■ ■ ■

Real golfers don't cry when they line up their fourth putt.

■ ■ ■

In a restaurant window: "Don't stand there and be hungry. Come on in and get fed up."

■ ■ ■

In the front yard of a funeral home: "Drive carefully. We'll wait."

■ ■ ■

Man: Are you certain this dog you're selling me is loyal?
Owner: Of course he sure is. I sold him five times, and every time he's come back.

■ ■ ■

A note left for a pianist from his wife: "Gone Chopin, have Liszt, Bach in a minuet."

■ ■ ■

Old skiers never die. They just go over the hill.

BONUS FUNNY

■ ■ ■

QUICK TAKES

Adam and Eve had an ideal marriage. He didn't have to hear about all the men she could have married, and she didn't have to hear about the way his mother cooked.

■ ■ ■

A Sunday school teacher asked her class why Joseph and Mary took Jesus with them to Jerusalem. A small child replied: "They couldn't get a babysitter."

■ ■ ■

A Sunday school teacher was discussing the Ten Commandments with her five- and six-year-olds. After explaining the commandment to "honor thy father and thy mother," she asked, "Is there a commandment that teaches us how to treat our brothers and sisters?" Without missing a beat, one little boy answered, "Thou shall not kill."

12. FAITH, HOPE, AND GIGGLES

Rejoice with those who rejoice.
ROMANS 12:15 NIV

I need to quit saying "stop me if I'm wrong"
because I'm never able to finish.
JON LAWHON

— — — — —

After a Sunday service, a burly visitor asked to speak with the minister's wife, who was well known for her charitable impulses.

"Madam," he said in a broken voice, "I wish to draw your attention to the terrible plight of a poor family in this neighborhood. The father is dead, the mother is too ill to work, and the seven children are starving. They are about to be turned out onto the cold, empty streets unless someone pays their rent—which amounts to $600."

"How terrible!" exclaimed the pastor's wife. "Thank you for bringing this to my attention. May I ask who you are?"

The sobbing visitor applied his handkerchief to his eyes. "I'm the landlord!"

A mother was preparing pancakes for her sons, Jack and Chris. The boys began to argue over who would get the first pancake. Their mother saw the opportunity for a moral lesson. "If Jesus were sitting here, He would say, 'Let My brother have the first pancake; I can wait.' "

Jack turned to his younger brother and said, "Chris, you be Jesus!"

■ ■ ■

A teenager was telling his pastor about their church's volunteer youth leader, who was refusing to allow the boy to join in any future camping trips.

"Why not?" the pastor asked. "What happened?"

"I think he's mad because I lost our compass when we waded through a creek," the boy replied.

"He's that mad," the pastor asked, "because a little compass got lost?"

"Well, it wasn't just the compass," the teen responded. "We all got lost."

■ ■ ■

Years ago, when our daughters were very young, we'd drop them off at our church's Children's Chapel on Sundays before the service.

One Sunday, just as I was about to open the door to the small chapel, the priest came rushing up in full vestments. He said he had an emergency and asked if I'd speak to the children at their story time. He said the subject was the twenty-third Psalm.

But just as I was about to get up from the back row and talk about the good shepherd, the priest burst into the room and signaled to me that he would be able to do the story time after all.

He told the children about sheep, that they weren't smart and needed lots of guidance, and that a shepherd's job was to stay close to the sheep, protect them from wild animals, and keep them from wandering off and doing dumb things that would get them hurt or killed.

He pointed to the little children in the room and said that they were the sheep and needed lots of guidance and protection.

Then the minister put his hands out to the side, palms up in a dramatic gesture, and with raised eyebrows said to the children, "If you are the sheep then who is the shepherd?" He was pretty obviously indicating himself.

A silence of a few seconds followed. Then a young visitor said, "Jesus, Jesus is the shepherd."

The young priest, obviously caught by surprise, said to the boy, "Well, then, who am I?"

The little boy frowned thoughtfully and then said with a shrug, "I guess you must be a sheepdog."

Q: Who was the greatest comedian in the Bible?
A: Samson. He brought the house down.

■ ■ ■

A nurse on the pediatric ward, before listening to the children's chests, would fit the stethoscope into their ears and let them listen to their own hearts. Their eyes would always light up with awe.

"Listen," she said to little four-year-old Seth, "Do you hear it? What do you suppose that is?"

He listened to the strange tap-tap-tapping deep in his chest. Then his eyes lit up, and he exclaimed, "Is that Jesus knocking?"

■ ■ ■

Two wicked brothers who were very wealthy used their money to cover up their evil ways. They went to the same church and appeared to be perfect Christian gentlemen. The elderly pastor of their church was not aware of their wickedness.

When the time came for the pastor to retire, a new pastor was hired who turned out to be very wise and intuitive. He saw right through the two brothers and didn't mind telling them so. The new pastor was a great preacher, and the church outgrew its old building. A campaign was started to raise funds for a new building.

Suddenly, one of the brothers died of a heart attack. The day before the funeral, the other brother went to the pastor and handed him a check for the entire amount needed to complete the building project. The pastor was stunned.

"I only have one condition," the evil brother said. "You must tell everyone that my brother was a saint during the funeral." The pastor nodded and slipped the check in his pocket.

At the funeral the next day, the pastor gave a full salvation message. Then he spoke about the deceased wicked man. "He was an evil man," the pastor said. "He used his money as a cover for his wickedness. He cheated and lied and swindled. But compared to his brother. . .he was a saint!"

■ ■ ■

A politician asked a minister, "What is something the government can do to help the church?"

"Well," the minister replied, "quit making one-dollar bills."

■ ■ ■

A vicar was talking to one of his parishioners. The vicar said, "When you get to my age you spend a lot more time thinking about the hereafter."

"How do you feel about that?" inquired the parishioner.

The vicar replied, "Well, I often find myself going into a room and thinking, *What did I come in here after?*"

A couple had two little boys, ages eight and ten, who were excessively mischievous. They were always getting into trouble, and their parents knew that, if any mischief occurred in their town, their sons were probably involved.

The boys' mother heard that a clergyman in town had been successful in disciplining children, so she asked if he would speak with her boys. The clergyman agreed, but asked to see them individually. So the mother sent her eight-year-old first, in the morning, with the older boy to see the clergyman in the afternoon.

The clergyman, a huge man with a booming voice, sat the younger boy down and asked him sternly, "Where is God?"

They boy's mouth dropped open, but he made no response, sitting there with his mouth hanging open, wide-eyed. So the clergyman repeated the question in an even sterner tone, "Where is God!!?" Again the boy made no attempt to answer. So the clergyman raised his voice even more and shook his finger in the boy's face and bellowed, "WHERE IS GOD!?"

The boy screamed and bolted from the room, ran directly home, and dove into his closet, slamming the door behind him. When his older brother found him in the closet, he asked, "What happened?"

The younger brother, gasping for breath,

replied, "We are in BIG trouble this time. God is missing—and they think WE did it!"

■ ■ ■

At a church dinner, there was a pile of apples on one end of a table with a sign that read, TAKE ONLY ONE APPLE, PLEASE. GOD IS WATCHING.

On the other end of the table was a pile of cookies where a youth had placed a sign saying, TAKE ALL THE COOKIES YOU WANT. GOD IS WATCHING THE APPLES.

■ ■ ■

The pastor spoke briefly, much to the delight of his audience.

■ ■ ■

Next Sunday, we will have a soloist for the morning service. Then the pastor will speak about "The Terrible Experience."

■ ■ ■

Ladies, don't forget the rummage sale. It is a good chance to get rid of those things not worth keeping around the house. Bring your husbands.

The pastor was just ending his children's sermon about heaven. After he prayed, he asked, "So kids, where do you want to go?"

"Heaven!" the kids yelled.

"And what do you have to be to get there?" asked the pastor.

"Dead!" shouted a little boy.

■ ■ ■

As a minister took his seat on a jet airplane, he noticed that the woman beside him had her Bible open and seemed to be reading it and praying fervently. As the plane taxied out to the runway, she appeared to become anxious. As the plane took off and gained altitude, she became more tense and grabbed the armrests tightly as sweat poured down her face. It was obvious that the higher the plane climbed, the more distressed the woman became.

Finally the pastor turned to comfort her. "There, there," he soothed, "you needn't be afraid. After all, remember that Jesus said, 'I am with you always.' "

"That's not what He said," the woman replied. "He said, '*Low*, I am with you always.' "

■ ■ ■

The Bible tells us that we should love our neighbors and our enemies. . .probably because they are usually the same people.

At a funeral the pastor was trying to explain that, although the body is dead, the soul has departed and gone on into eternity.

"What you see here is just the shell," he said. "The nut has departed."

■ ■ ■

Q: What excuse did Adam give to his children as to why he no longer lived in Eden?
A: Your mother ate us out of house and home.

■ ■ ■

The minister of a small church knew that improvements were needed on the church building. He suggested purchasing a chandelier, but the church members voted it down.

"Why are you opposed to buying a chandelier?" the preacher questioned.

"First, no one can spell it," said the spokesperson. "Second, no one can play it. And finally, what we really need is more light."

■ ■ ■

The class on prophecy has been canceled due to unforeseen circumstances.

A man dies and goes to heaven where Peter meets him at the pearly gates. Peter says, "You need a thousand points to make it into heaven. You tell me all the good things you've done, and I give you a certain number of points for each item. When you reach one thousand points, you get in."

"Okay," the man says, "I was happily married to the same woman for fifty years and never cheated on her, not even in my mind."

"That's wonderful," says Peter, "that's worth two points!"

"Two points?" he says. "Well, I attended church all my life and gave my ten percent tithe faithfully."

"Terrific!" says Peter. "That's definitely worth a point."

"One point? My goodness! Well, what about this? I started a soup kitchen in my city and worked in a shelter for the homeless."

"Fantastic, that's good for two more points," he says.

"Two points!" the man cries. "At this rate, the only way I can get into heaven is by the grace of God!"

"Now that's what we're looking for! Come on in!"

A pastor and a couple of deacons were standing by the side of the road, pounding a sign into the ground that read: THE END IS NEAR! TURN YOURSELF AROUND NOW—BEFORE IT'S TOO LATE!

A car raced past, and the indignant driver yelled, "Leave us alone, you religious nuts!" From the curve they heard screeching tires and a big splash.

The pastor turned to a deacon and asked, "Do you think maybe we should have just written 'Bridge Out' on our sign?"

■ ■ ■

The cost for attending the fasting and prayer conference includes meals.

■ ■ ■

Johnny had been misbehaving and was sent to his room. After a while he emerged and informed his mother that he had thought it over and then said a prayer.

"Fine," said the pleased mother. "If you ask God to help you not misbehave, He will help you."

"Oh, I didn't ask Him to help me not misbehave," said Johnny. "I asked Him to help you put up with me."

One cold winter day, a boy was standing outside a shoe store, praying to God for some socks or some shoes. Just then a lady walked up to him and said, "Is there something that I can help you with?"

He looked down at his feet and said, "Well, I would like some shoes."

She grabbed his hand and took him into the shoe store. She asked for a dozen pairs of socks and a pair of shoes. They sat down, and the clerk put a pair of socks and shoes on the boy.

As the woman got up to leave, the boy thanked her. She told him that if he ever needed anything else, to not to be afraid to ask.

He looked at her and asked, "Are you God's wife?"

■ ■ ■

A little boy's prayer. "Dear God, please take care of my daddy and my mommy and my sister and my brother and my doggy and me. Oh, please take care of Yourself, God. If anything happens to You, we're gonna be in a big mess."

One Sunday in a Midwest city a young child was "acting up" during the morning worship hour. The parents did their best to maintain some sense of order in the pew but were losing the battle. Finally the father picked the little fellow up and walked sternly up the aisle on his way out. Just before reaching the safety of the foyer the little one called loudly to the congregation, "Pray for me! Pray for me!"

■ ■ ■

Q: What was the greatest female financier in the Bible?
A: Pharaoh's daughter. She went down to the bank of the Nile and drew out little prophet.

■ ■ ■

A bean supper will be held on Wednesday evening in the church hall. Music will follow.

■ ■ ■

A pastor was preaching about Judgment Day. "Thunder will roar, flames will flash across the sky. Floods, storms, devastation such as you've never seen. . ." he continued dramatically.

Wide eyed, a young boy turned to his mother. "Will I get to skip school that day?" he whispered.

Abraham decided to upgrade his old computer to the new version of Windows. Isaac couldn't believe it.

"Dad, your old PC doesn't have enough memory!"

"My son," Abraham responded, "God Himself will provide the RAM."

■ ■ ■

After a church service, three boys were bragging about their fathers.

The first boy said, "My dad scribbles a few words on a piece of paper, calls it a poem, and gets fifty dollars for it."

The second boy said, "That's nothing—my dad scribbles a few words on a piece of paper, calls it a song, and he gets a hundred dollars."

The third boy said, "I've got you both beat. My dad scribbles a few words on a piece of paper, calls it a sermon, and it takes four people to collect all the money!"

■ ■ ■

A Bible study group was discussing the unforeseen possibility of sudden death. "We will all die someday," the leader of the discussion said, "and none of us really knows when, but if we did, we would all do a better job of preparing ourselves for that day." Everybody nodded their heads in agreement with this comment.

"What would you do if you knew you only had four weeks of life left before your great Judgment Day?" the leader asked the group.

"For those four weeks, I would go out into my community and witness to those that have not yet accepted Jesus into their lives," one person said.

"A very wise thing to do," said the group leader. And all the group members agreed that would be a very good thing to do.

"For those four weeks, I would dedicate all my remaining time to being of more service to others," said another woman.

"That's wonderful!" the group leader commented, and all the group members agreed.

One gentleman in the back finally spoke up loudly. "For those four weeks, I would travel throughout the United States with my mother-in-law in an economy car and stay in a cheap motel every night."

Everyone was puzzled by his answer. "Why would you do that?" the group leader asked curiously.

"Because"—the man smiled sarcastically—"it would be the longest four weeks of my life."

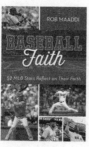